INTRODUCING
MATH!
GRADE 7

ARGOPREP

FREE VIDEO EXPLANATIONS

600 QUESTIONS TO PRACTICE

TEACHER RECOMMENDED

TOPICS COVERED

PRACTICE MAKES PERFECT

- Ratios & Proportional Relationships
- The Number System
- Expressions and Equations
- Statistics & Probability
- Geometry

ArgoPrep is one of the leading providers of supplemental educational products and services. We offer affordable and effective test prep solutions to educators, parents and students. Learning should be fun and easy! For that reason, most of our workbooks come with detailed video answer explanations taught by one of our fabulous instructors.

Our goal is to make your life easier, so let us know how we can help you by e-mailing us at: info@argoprep.com.

Aknowlegments:

Icons made by Freepik, Creaticca Creative Agency, Pixel perfect , Pixel Buddha, Smashicons, Twitter , Good Ware, Smalllikeart, Nikita Golubev, monkik, DinosoftLabs, Icon Pond from www.flaticon.com

TABLE OF CONTENTS

Chapter 1 - Ratios & Proportional Relationships 10
1.1. Compute Unit Rates. 12
1.2. Recognize and represent proportional relationships between quantities 20
1.3. Solving multi-step ratio and percent problems... 29
1.4. Chapter Test 38

Chapter 2 - The Number System. 46
2.1. Apply and extend previous understandings of operations with fractions. 48
2.2. Apply and extend previous understandings of multiplication and division. 57
2.3. Solve real-world problems involving the four operations. 63
2.4. Chapter Test. 70

Chapter 3 - Expressions and Equations 78
3.1. Use properties of operations to generate equivalent expressions 80
3.2. Solve real-life and mathematical problems using numerical and algebraic
expressions and equations.. 98
3.3. Chapter Test. 116

Chapter 4 - Geometry. 124
4.1. Draw construct, and describe geometrical figures and describe the
relationships between them.. 126
4.2. Solve real-life and mathematical problems involving angle measure,
area, surface area, and volume.. 150
4.3. Chapter Test. 172

Chapter 5 - Statistics & Probability. 180
5.1. Use random sampling to draw inferences about a population.. 182
5.2. Draw informal comparative inferences about two populations.. 201
5.3. Investigate chance processes and develop, use, and evaluate
probability models. 219
5.4. Chapter Test. 243

Chapter 6 - Mixed Assessment 254

Answer Key 296

HOW TO USE
THE BOOK

Welcome to the Introducing Math! series by ArgoPrep.

This workbook is designed to provide you with a comprehensive overview of Grade 7 mathematics.

While working through this workbook, be sure to read the topic overview that will give you a general foundation of the concept. At the end of each chapter, there is a chapter test that will assess how well you understood the topics presented.

This workbook comes with free digital video explanations that you can access on our website. If you are unsure on how to answer a question, we strongly recommend watching the video explanations as it will reinforce the fundamental concepts.

We strive to provide you with an amazing learning experience. If you have any suggestions or need further assistance, don't hesitate to email us at info@argoprep.com or chat with us live on our website at www.argoprep.com

HOW TO WATCH
VIDEO EXPLANATIONS
IT IS ABSOLUTELY FREE

Step 1 - Visit our website at: www.argoprep.com/k8

Step 2 - Click on the JOIN FOR FREE button located on the top right corner.

Step 3 - Choose the grade level workbook you have.

Step 4 - Sign up as a Learner, Parent or a Teacher.

Step 5 - Register using your email or social networks.

Step 6 - From your dashboard cick on FREE WORKBOOKS EXPLANATION on the left and choose the workbook you have.

You now have life time access to the video explanations for your workbook!

OTHER BOOKS BY ARGOPREP

Here are some other test prep workbooks by ArgoPrep you may be interested in. All of our workbooks come equipped with detailed video explanations to make your learning experience a breeze! Visit us at www.argoprep.com

COMMON CORE SERIES

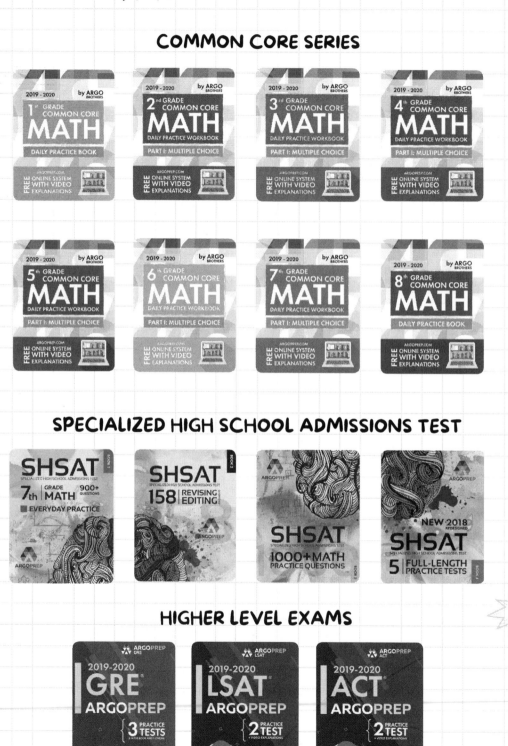

SPECIALIZED HIGH SCHOOL ADMISSIONS TEST

HIGHER LEVEL EXAMS

INTRODUCING MATH!

Introducing Math! by ArgoPrep is an award-winning series created by certified teachers to provide students with high-quality practice problems. Our workbooks include topic overviews with instruction, practice questions, answer explanations along with digital access to video explanations. Practice in confidence - with ArgoPrep!

YOGA MINDFULNESS

If you are looking for a fun way to engage with your children while helping them build a mindful, engaged and healthy lifestyle, Frogyogi's Yoga Stories for Kids and Parents is the perfect book for you and your family!

KIDS SUMMER ACADEMY SERIES

ArgoPrep's **Kids Summer Academy** series helps prevent summer learning loss and gets students ready for their new school year by reinforcing core foundations in math, english and science. Our workbooks also introduce new concepts so students can get a head start and be on top of their game for the new school year!

Meet the ArgoPrep heroes.

Are you ready to go on an incredible adventure and complete your journey with them to become a **SUPER** student?

Chapter 1:
Ratios & Proportional Relationships

1.1. Compute Unit Rates page 12

1.2. Recognize and represent proportional relationships between quantities. page 20

1.3. Solving multi-step ratio and percent problems. page 29

1.4. Chapter Test page 38

ARGOPREP

You have spent years as a student exploring fractions. As you get older, you can see more and more applications for fractions in the real world. This chapter, we are going to examine **how what we know about fractions can apply to rates and ratios**.

Remember a unit rate represents the amount of something that occurs in one unit. For example, your car speed is calculated at a unit rate of miles per hour.

You can translate information into a unit rate. For example, our school has **90 kids** and **5 classrooms**. What is the unit rate of kids per classroom? The easiest way to find this is to simplify the fraction.

$$\text{So, } \frac{90}{5} = \frac{?}{1}$$

To simplify **5** to **1**, you divide by **5**. So to simplify the top, you also need to divide by **5**.

When you do this, you get an answer of **16**.

You can use rates to solve problems. Let's use the unit rate above.

If there is **1 classroom** for every **16 kids** and each classroom has a total of **12 computers**, how may kids are there per computer?

$$\frac{\text{1 classroom}}{16 \text{ kids}} \times \frac{12 \text{ computers}}{\text{1 classroom}} = \frac{12 \text{ computers}}{16 \text{ kids}} = \frac{3 \text{ computers}}{4 \text{ kids}}$$

You solve this problem by setting up multiple ratios and reducing/canceling appropriate numbers. The rate ends up being computers per kids as both classrooms cancel. Then you divide **12** and **16,** both by **4**, ending up with **3** on the numerator and **4** in the denominator.

You can also calculate answers using unit rates. For example, $\frac{1}{4}$ of the students in each classroom above walk home from school. How many students walk home from school?

To solve this, you take $\frac{1}{4}$ of 16 or multiply $\frac{1}{4} \times \frac{16}{1}$, which would give you an answer of 4.

1. Morgan buys $4\frac{1}{3}$ cartons of apples for $39. How much does 1 carton of apples cost?

A. $4

B. $10

C. $8

D. $9

SHOW YOUR WORK

$\frac{13}{3}$ $\frac{1}{x}$ $\frac{13}{3} \times 39$

$\frac{13 \times = 117}{13}$ $\frac{12}{9}$

$1x = 9$

2. If there are 64 cars on 4 roads, what is the unit rate of cars per road?

A. 16 roads/car

B. 16 cars/road

C. 1 car/8 roads

D. 8 roads/1 car

SHOW YOUR WORK

$64 \div 4 =$

16

3. Our family's car can drive **396** miles on 1 tank of gas. If the tank holds **12** gallons, what is the unit rate of miles per gallon?

A. 22 gallons/mile

B. 22 miles/gallon

C. 33 miles/gallon

D. 33 gallons/mile

SHOW YOUR WORK

396 ÷ 12 = 33

4. There are **705** tickets sold for **3** concerts. What is the unit rate of tickets per concert?

A. 235 tickets/concert

B. 235 concerts/ticket

C. 253 concerts/ticket

D. 253 concerts/ticket

SHOW YOUR WORK

705 ÷ 3 = 235

5. **450** people travel from one city to another on **6** planes. What is the unit rate of people per plane?

A. 75 planes/person

B. 75 people/plane

C. 25 people/plane

D. 150 people/plane

SHOW YOUR WORK

450 ÷ 6 = 75

6. Alicia rented a car for a total cost of **$380** for $2\frac{1}{2}$ days. What was the cost of the car per day?

  A. $56/day

  B. $66/ day

  C. $152/ day

  D. $86 / day

SHOW YOUR WORK

$380 \div 2.5 = 152$

7. Sarah waters $\frac{1}{3}$ of her garden in $\frac{1}{2}$ of an hour. How much of her garden does she water in an hour?

  A. $\frac{3}{4}$ of her garden

  B. $\frac{1}{6}$ of her garden

  C. The whole garden

  D. $\frac{2}{3}$ of her garden

SHOW YOUR WORK

$\dfrac{\frac{1}{3}}{\frac{1}{2}} = \dfrac{x}{1}$

$\frac{1}{2} = \frac{1}{3}(2)$

$1x = \frac{2}{3}$

45m

8. Edward runs $\frac{1}{3}$ of a mile in **5** minutes. If he runs $\frac{3}{4}$ of an hour total, how far does he go?

  A. 6 miles

  B. 3 miles

  C. 12 miles

  D. 9 miles

SHOW YOUR WORK

miles: $\dfrac{\frac{1}{3}}{5} = \dfrac{x}{45}$

minutes:

$\frac{5x}{5} = \frac{15}{5}$

$x = 3$

$\frac{45}{1} \times \frac{1}{3} = 45$

$x = 3$

9. Brian reads $\frac{4}{5}$ of a chapter in $\frac{1}{4}$ of an hour. If his book has 10 chapters, how much

of the book does he read in 3 hours?

A. $9\frac{3}{5}$ chapters

B. $9\frac{1}{5}$ chapters

C. $9\frac{4}{5}$ chapters

D. 10 chapters

SHOW YOUR WORK

$$\frac{4}{5} \times \frac{1}{3}$$

$$\frac{1}{4}$$

$$1x = \frac{48}{5}$$

$$(4) \frac{1}{4}x = \frac{12}{5}$$

$$\frac{3}{1} \times \frac{4}{5} = \frac{12}{5}$$

$$9\frac{3}{5}$$

$$(4) = \frac{48}{5}$$

$$5\overline{)48}$$

$$\frac{45}{3}$$

10. Which ratio is $\frac{16}{24}$ in simplest form?

A. $\frac{4}{5}$

B. $\frac{2}{3}$

C. $\frac{3}{2}$

D. $\frac{1}{2}$

SHOW YOUR WORK

$$\frac{16}{24} = \frac{2}{3}$$

11. Which ratio is $\frac{99}{63}$ in simplest form?

A. $\frac{7}{9}$

B. $\frac{9}{11}$

C. $\frac{11}{7}$

D. $\frac{9}{7}$

SHOW YOUR WORK

$$99 \div 9 = \frac{11}{7}$$
$$63 \div 9 = 7$$

12. Our family likes many different pizza toppings. To make everyone happy, we order 1 pizza with $\frac{1}{3}$ pepperoni and $\frac{1}{3}$ sausage. We order another pizza with $\frac{1}{2}$ pepperoni and sausage. If each pizza is cut into **6** pieces, how many total pieces have meat toppings?

A. 4

B. 5

C. 6

(D.) 7

SHOW YOUR WORK

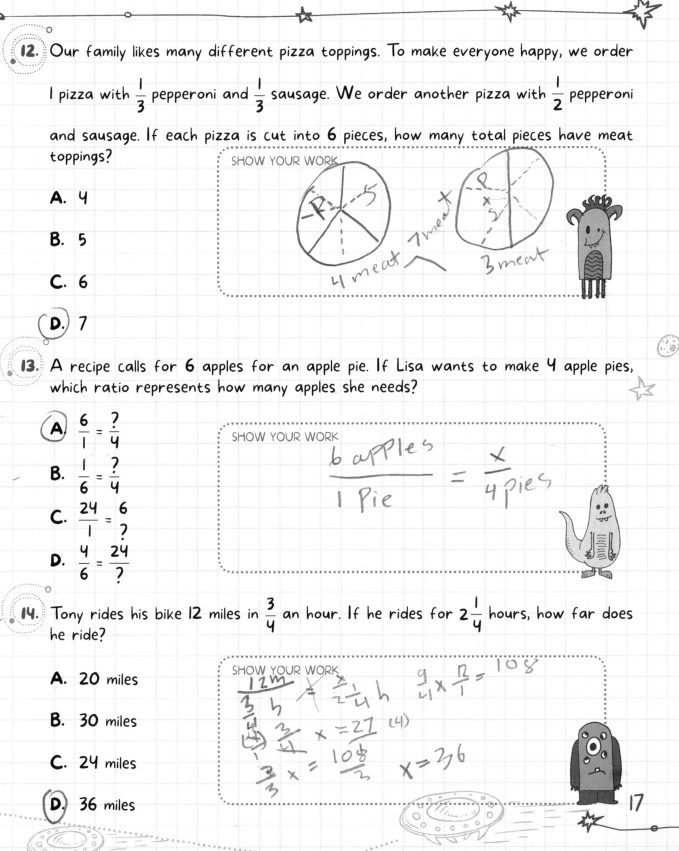

13. A recipe calls for **6** apples for an apple pie. If Lisa wants to make **4** apple pies, which ratio represents how many apples she needs?

(A.) $\frac{6}{1} = \frac{?}{4}$

B. $\frac{1}{6} = \frac{?}{4}$

C. $\frac{24}{1} = \frac{6}{?}$

D. $\frac{4}{6} = \frac{24}{?}$

SHOW YOUR WORK

$$\frac{6\ apples}{1\ Pie} = \frac{x}{4\ pies}$$

14. Tony rides his bike 12 miles in $\frac{3}{4}$ an hour. If he rides for $2\frac{1}{4}$ hours, how far does he ride?

A. 20 miles

B. 30 miles

C. 24 miles

(D.) 36 miles

SHOW YOUR WORK

17

ARGOPREP

15. John mows $\frac{1}{3}$ of his lawn in **30** minutes. How long does it take him to mow his whole law?

A. 45 minutes

B. 1 hour

C. $1\frac{1}{2}$ hours

D. 2 hours

SHOW YOUR WORK

$\frac{\frac{1}{3}}{30} = \frac{\frac{1}{x}}{x}$ $(3)\frac{1}{3}x = 30 \times 3 = 90$

$x = 90$

16. A **3** pound bag of apples costs **$6**. If there are about **8** apples in a pound, how much would 1 apple cost?

A. 12 cents

B. 25 cents

C. 50 cents

D. $1

SHOW YOUR WORK

$\frac{3}{6} = \frac{1}{x}$

$\frac{3}{3}x = \frac{6}{3}$

$x = 2$

$8\overline{)2.00}$ 25
$\underline{16}$
40

25 cents

17. Evan swims $\frac{1}{2}$ of a mile in $\frac{1}{4}$ of an hour. How far will he swim in **45** minutes?

A. $\frac{3}{4}$ miles

B. $1\frac{1}{2}$ miles

C. 1 mile

D. 2 miles

SHOW YOUR WORK

$\frac{\frac{1}{2}}{\frac{1}{4}} = \frac{x}{\frac{3}{4}}$

$(4)\frac{1}{4} = \frac{3}{8}(4)$

$x = \frac{12}{8} = 1\frac{1}{2}$

$1\frac{1}{2}$

ARGOPREP

18. Using the formula, speed = distance/time, how fast are you going if it takes you $\frac{1}{4}$ of an hour to go $\frac{2}{3}$ of a mile?

A. $2\frac{2}{3}$ miles/hour

B. 3 miles/hour

C. 2 miles/hour

D. 4 miles/hour

SHOW YOUR WORK

$\frac{\frac{2}{3}}{\frac{1}{4}}$ $\frac{2}{3} \times \frac{4}{1} = \frac{8}{3}$ $3\sqrt{\frac{8}{6}}$ $\frac{-6}{2}$

$2\frac{2}{3}$

19. Sydney is taking a bike ride. She rides 4.8 miles in 3 hours. How far does she go in 1 hour?

A. 4 miles

B. 2 miles

C. 3.2 miles

D. 1.6 miles

SHOW YOUR WORK

$\frac{4.8}{3} = \frac{x}{1-h}$

$\frac{3}{3}x = \frac{4.8}{3}$

$x = 1.6$

$3\overline{)4.8}$ 1.6
$\frac{-3}{18}$
$\frac{18}{0}$

20. Bailey walks his dog every day. They travel a total of 1.25 miles in 45 minutes each day. How far do they go in 4 days?

A. 200 miles

B. 10 miles

C. 5 miles

D. 300 miles

SHOW YOUR WORK

$\frac{miles\ 1.25}{minutes\ 45} = \frac{x}{180\ minutes}$

$\frac{45}{45} = \frac{225}{45}$

$x = 5$

$45 \times 4 = 180$

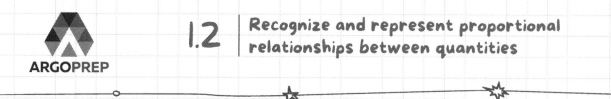
Do you remember how to define a proportional relationship? A relationship is proportional if two quantities vary directly by each other. A proportional relationship is usually represented by the equation, $y = kx$, where k is the **constant**.

Let's look at an example. $y = 5x$

If we are to fill out a table of values that represent the proportional relationship of $y = 5x$, it would look like the following:

x	y
1	5
2	10
3	15
4	20
5	25

This can also be represented on a graph. See the model below:

We can use the information we have about proportional relationships to identify the constant rate. If we are given the x and y values of a set of points, we can use those values to calculate how the x and y values are related.

For example,

x	y
1	3
2	6
5	15
7	21
9	27

Although the x values do not have any particular order of increase, we can see a pattern between the x and y values. Each y value is **3 times** its x value. That makes the constant for this relationship **3** so the equation would be $y = 3x$.

Graphs on the coordinate plane help us examine these relationships closely.

Let's take a look at an example.

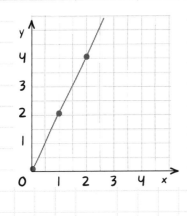

Graphs that display proportional relationships are called direct variation graphs because y varies directly with x based on the constant, k. These graphs have a couple of key factors.

First, these graphs always go through the origin, **(0,0)**. This is because when we plug in **0** for x, anything multiplied by **0** is **0**.

Second, the value for x = 1 is always the value of the constant. This is because anything **times 1** is itself.

Any point on the graph can be calculated by multiplying the x value by the constant to determine the y.

1. Which answer would be a correct value for y in the equation $y = 8x$ if $x = 4$?

    A. 32

    B. 4

    C. 12

    D. 24

    SHOW YOUR WORK

    $8 \times 4 = 32$

2. Which answer would be a correct value for x in the equation $y = 4x$ if $y = 28$?

    A. 4

    B. 5

    C. 6

    D. 7

    SHOW YOUR WORK

    $4 \times 7 = 28$

3. What is the constant rate for these values?

(2, 8) (4, 16) (10, 40)

A. 2

B. 4

C. 8

D. 10

SHOW YOUR WORK

$2 \times 4 = 8$
$4 \times 4 = 16$
$10 \times 4 = 40$

4. What is the constant rate for these values?

(3, 30) (7, 70) (9, 90)

A. 6

B. 8

C. 10

D. 12

SHOW YOUR WORK

$3 \times 10 = 30$
$7 \times 10 = 70$
$9 \times 10 = 90$

5. What is the constant rate for these values?

x	y
2	10
4	20
6	30

SHOW YOUR WORK

$2 \times 5 = 10$
$4 \times 5 = 20$
$6 \times 5 = 30$

A. 5   B. 2   C. 10   D. 8

23

6. What is the constant rate for these values?

x	y
6	66
8	88
11	121

SHOW YOUR WORK

A. 8   B. 9   C. 10   D. 11

7. If the relationship is represented by the equation y = 8x, and x = 7, what is y?

A. 24

B. 56

C. 8

D. 7

SHOW YOUR WORK

$8 \times 7 = 56$

8. If the relationship is represented by the equation y = 5x, and x = 11, what is y?

A. 40

B. 45

C. 50

D. 55

SHOW YOUR WORK

9. If the relationship is represented by the equation $y=6x$, and $y=36$, what is x?

A. 4

B. 5

C. 6

D. 7

SHOW YOUR WORK

10. If the relationship is represented by the equation $y = 7x$, and $x = 12$, what is y?

A. 86

B. 84

C. 82

D. 80

SHOW YOUR WORK

11. If the point (4, 36) is found on the line $y = kx$, what is k?

x y

A. 6

B. 7

C. 8

D. 9

SHOW YOUR WORK

$$36 = K4$$

12. If the point (6, 48) is found on the line $y = kx$, what is k?

A. 8

B. 7

C. 6

D. 5

SHOW YOUR WORK

$48 = k6$

13. Which point always will be a part of a line represented by $y = kx$?

A. (0, 0)

B. (1, 1)

C. (2, 2)

D. (1, 2)

SHOW YOUR WORK

14. In any line $y=kx$, the y value at $x = 1$ will always equal what?

A. 1

B. 0

C. y

D. k

SHOW YOUR WORK

15. If you were to graph the line y = 9x, which point would fall on the line?

A. (5, 4)

B. (5, 14)

C. (5, 45)

D. (5, 9)

SHOW YOUR WORK

4 = 9

4x 5 = 45

16. If you were to graph the line y = 20x, which point would fall on the line?

A. (1, 10)

B. (3, 60)

C. (2, 10)

D. (3, 30)

SHOW YOUR WORK

17. If you were to graph the line y = 4x, which point would fall on the line?

A. (6, 24)

B. (6, 10)

C. (6, 2)

D. (6, 14)

SHOW YOUR WORK

18. If you were to graph the line y = **5x**, which point would fall on the line?

A. (3, 15)

B. (15, 3)

C. (3, 8)

D. (3, 5)

SHOW YOUR WORK

19. If you were to graph the line y = **7x**, which point would fall on the line?

A. (7, 11)

B. (7, 7)

C. (7, 49)

D. (7, 42)

SHOW YOUR WORK

20. If you were to graph the line y = **12x**, which point would fall on the line?

A. (12, 1)

B. (2, 12)

C. (6, 12)

D. (1, 12)

SHOW YOUR WORK

We can use our knowledge of proportions to solve problems involving percents. This is because **percents can be represented as a proportion of the percent over 100**.

Let's look at a few examples!

Simple interest is calculated by the formula, Interest = **Principle x Rate x Time**.

Calculate the interest gained on an account that starts with **$400** at a rate of **3%** a year over **5 years**.

First, you need **to set up proportions** to solve this problem.

Using the formula, Interest = **Principle x Rate x Time**, your problem becomes

$$I = 400 \times \frac{3}{100} \times 5$$

$$\frac{400 \times 3 \times 5}{100} = 60$$

To calculate how much money would be gained over **5 years**, you add that back to the original amount. 400 + 60 = **$460**.

Let's look at another example!

A store is having a sale and reduces it items by **25%**. Teddy is interested in buying a hat that was originally priced at **$36**. What is its new cost?

First, you need to calculate **25%** of **36**.

You can solve this problem by using a proportion.

$$\frac{25}{100} \times \frac{36}{1} = \$9$$

$$\frac{25 \cdot 000}{100 \, \$} = \frac{x}{36}$$

$$\frac{900}{100} = \frac{100x}{100}$$

$$9 = x$$

29

Then, you subtract the markdown from the original amount. **36 - 9 = $25.** ✓

We can use percents to see how <u>accurate</u> our estimates are. Let's see how that works.

When planning for a race, the committee planned for **225** people. Only **175** people came. What was the percent error of the committee?

First you need to determine the difference between the original estimate and the actual amount.

225 - 175 = 50

Then, you take that amount and place it over the actual value.

$\frac{50}{175}$ = **0.2857**

To get the percentage, you multiply by **100**.

The percentage of error of the committee was **29%** (amount was **28.57**, which we rounded to **29**).

NOTES

1. Calculate the interest gained on an account that starts with **$75** at a rate of **1%** a year over **5** years.

A. $1.50

B. $3.75

C. $2.25

D. $4.50

SHOW YOUR WORK

$$I = \frac{75}{1} \times \frac{1}{100} \times \frac{5}{1}$$

$$\begin{array}{r} 75 \\ \times\ 3\ 5 \\ \hline \$\ 375 \end{array}$$

2. How much money would be in an account that starts with **$125** and earns **2%** interest a year over **3** years?

A. $5.25

B. $7.50

C. $132.50

D. $133.75

SHOW YOUR WORK

$$I = \frac{125}{1} \times \frac{2}{100} \times \frac{3}{1}$$

7.50

3. Laura buys **$60** worth of baby clothes. She has to pay **4%** tax on her purchase. What will be her total bill?

A. $64.20

B. $63.00

C. $62.00

D. $62.40

SHOW YOUR WORK

$$I = 60 \cdot 1.04$$

$$\frac{60}{1} \cdot \frac{104}{100} = \frac{6240}{100} = 62.40$$

$$\begin{array}{r} 1.04 \\ \times\ 60 \\ \hline 6240 \end{array}$$

$1\frac{4}{100}$

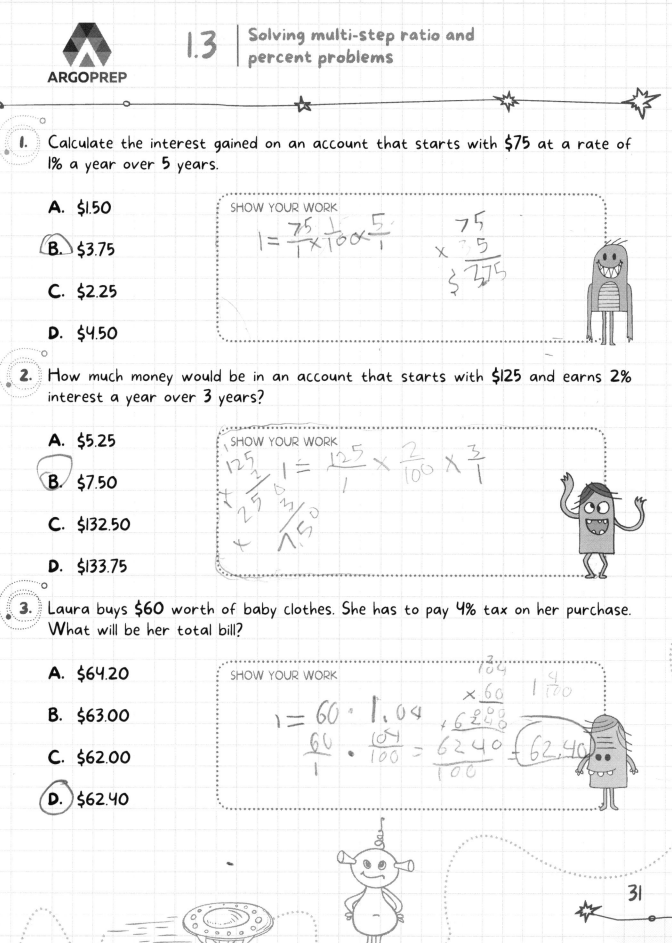

31

4. Liam buys **$220** worth of groceries. He has to pay **6%** tax on his purchase. He has **$230**. Does he have enough money to make his purchase? Explain your response.

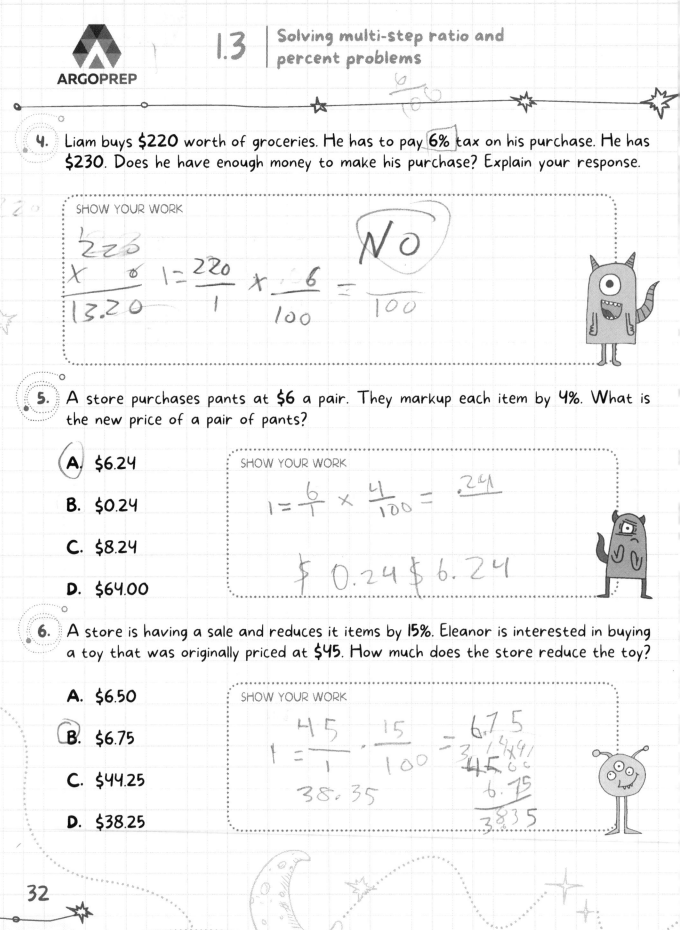

SHOW YOUR WORK

$$\frac{220}{13.20} \quad 1 = \frac{220}{1} \times \frac{6}{100} = \frac{}{100}$$

$\times$ 6

NO

5. A store purchases pants at **$6** a pair. They markup each item by **4%**. What is the new price of a pair of pants?

A. $6.24

B. $0.24

C. $8.24

D. $64.00

SHOW YOUR WORK

$$1 = \frac{6}{1} \times \frac{4}{100} = .24$$

$ 0.24 $ 6.24

6. A store is having a sale and reduces it items by **15%**. Eleanor is interested in buying a toy that was originally priced at **$45**. How much does the store reduce the toy?

A. $6.50

B. $6.75

C. $44.25

D. $38.25

SHOW YOUR WORK

$$1 = \frac{45}{1} \cdot \frac{15}{100} = \frac{6.75}{3}$$

38.35

45.00
6.75
3835

7. Mary and her three friends go out to lunch and their bill is **$36**. If they want to tip their waitress the standard **15%**, how much money should they tip?

A. $4.50

B. $5.00

C. $5.40

D. $6.00

SHOW YOUR WORK

$$1 = \frac{36}{1} \times \frac{15}{100}$$

$5.40

8. Logan and his two friends go out to dinner and their bill is **$33**. If they want to tip their server the standard **15%** and want to split the bill evenly, how much will each friend pay?

A. $9.40

B. $9.45

C. $12.65

D. $12.60

SHOW YOUR WORK

$$1 = \frac{33}{1} \times \frac{15}{100} = 4.95$$

9. A realtor earns **3%** commission on any house sale she makes. If she sells a house for **$125,000**, how much commission is she going to earn?

A. $375,000

B. $375

C. $3,570

D. $3,750

SHOW YOUR WORK

$$1 = \frac{125,000}{1} \times \frac{3}{100}$$

3,750

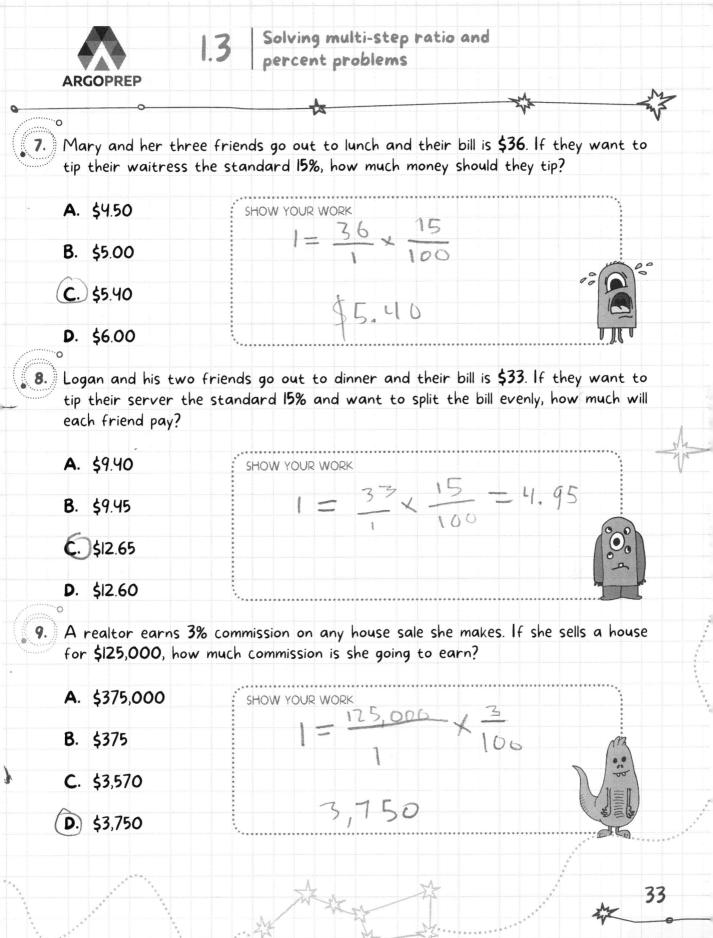

10. A realtor earns **3%** commission on any house sale he makes. If he sells a house for **$85,000**, how much commission is he going to earn?

A. $2,000

B. $2,550

C. $2,500

D. $2,600

SHOW YOUR WORK

$1 = \dfrac{85,000}{1} \times \dfrac{3}{100} =$

2,550

11. Maria gets a new cell phone and has to pay **$15/month** plus a **$65** start-up fee. How much money will she pay in **6** months?

A. $155

B. $165

C. $175

D. $185

SHOW YOUR WORK

$1 = 65 + \dfrac{15}{1} \times \dfrac{6}{1}$

12. Tad joins a gym and has to pay a membership fee of **$20** in addition to **$8** a month? How much will his membership cost after **8** months?

A. $78

B. $80

C. $82

D. $84

SHOW YOUR WORK

$1 = 20 + \dfrac{8}{1} \times \dfrac{8}{1} = \$84$

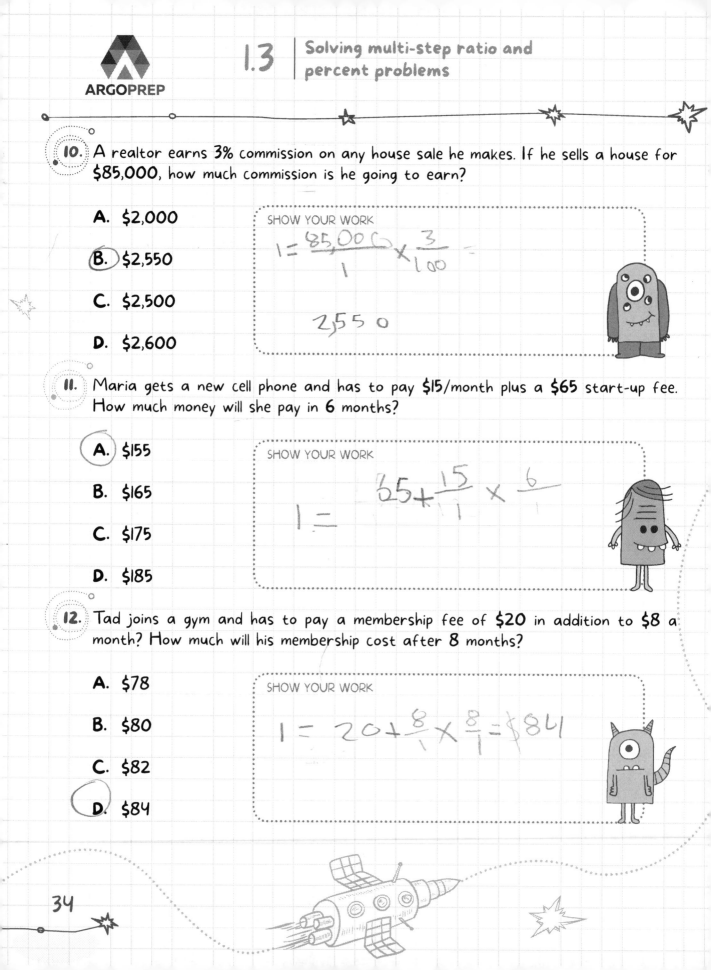

13. The enrollment in a dance school increases from **65** to **85** in three years. What is it's percent increase, assuming it grows at a constant rate?

A. 30%

B. 31%

C. 32%

D. 33%

SHOW YOUR WORK

85
− 65
20

$\frac{20}{65} = .3076^{9}$
↓
31%

14. A rare toy is bought at a store for **$48**. After five years, it is worth **$250**. What is its percent increase?

x=131
=131%

A. 42.1%

B. 4.21%

C. 421%

D. 100%

SHOW YOUR WORK

250
− 48
202

202 ÷ 48 = 4.21
4.21 × 100
↓
421

15. The price of a car decreases from **$24,000** to **$22,000**. What is the percent decrease?

A. 8.3%

B. 83%

C. 830%

D. 20%

SHOW YOUR WORK

24,000 − 22,000 = 2,000

$\frac{2,000}{24,000}$ = .0830 × 100

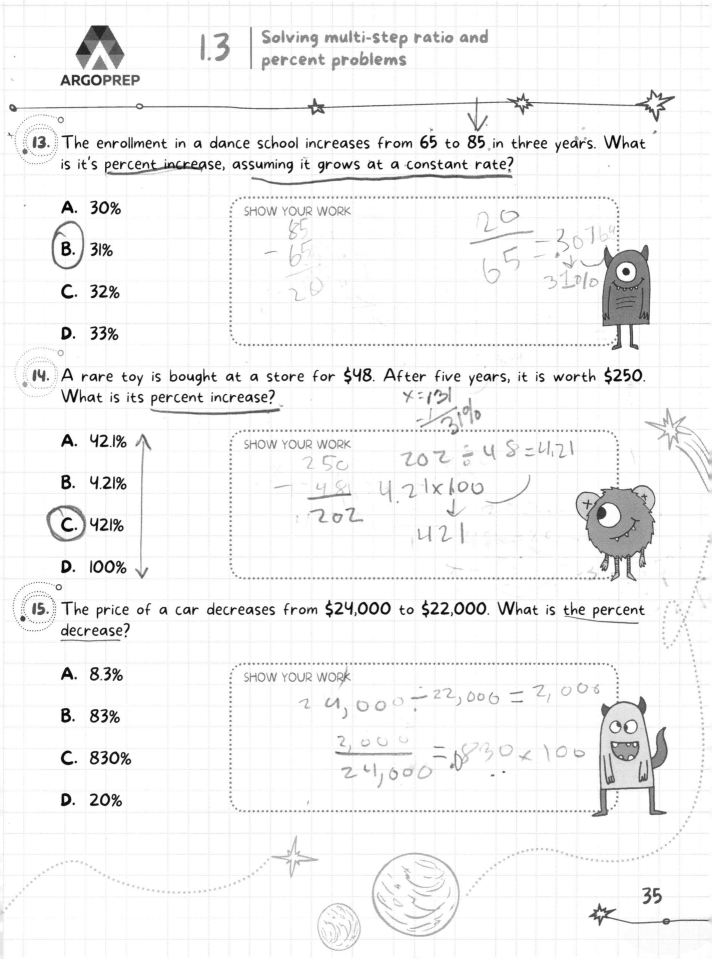

35

101, .054, 1000

16. A seller decreases the listed price of his home from **$275,000** to **$260,000**. What is his <u>percent decrease?</u>

A. 0.54%

B. 5.4%

C. 54%

D. 55%

SHOW YOUR WORK

275,000 − 260,000 = 15,000

$$\frac{15,000}{275,000} = 0.05454$$

0.05...

17. Matthew estimates a book will take him **2** weeks (14 days) to read. It actually takes him **15** days. What is his <u>percent error?</u>

INCREASE

A. 4%

B. 5%

C. 6%

D. 7%

SHOW YOUR WORK

$$\frac{1}{14} = .0714$$

18. Our science class completes an experiment. We estimate it will **3** weeks for a plant to grow to a certain height but it actually takes **28** days. What is our percent error?

A. 3%

B. $\frac{1}{3}$

C. 33%

D. 13%

SHOW YOUR WORK

$$\frac{7}{21} = 0.333$$

33%

19. Mrs. Daniels estimates that 72 people will come to the music concert. 95 people actually attend. What is her percent error?

A. 130%

B. 131%

C. 31.9%

D. 349%

SHOW YOUR WORK

20. How much money would be in an account that starts with $145 and earns 3% interest a year over 8 years?

A. $179.80

B. $34.80

C. $200

D. $185

SHOW YOUR WORK

NOTES

1. A store has a sale of 4 bags of cookies for $12.00. What is the unit rate?

   A. 4 cookies/$1

   B. $4/bag of cookies

   C. $6/bag of cookies

   D. $3/bag of cookies

SHOW YOUR WORK

$12 \div 4 = 3$

2. Alicia types 250 words per 10 minutes. How many words can she type per minute?

   A. 25 minutes/word

   B. 25 words/minute

   C. 4 words/minute

   D. 4 minutes/word

SHOW YOUR WORK

$250 \div 10 = 25$

3. Which ratio is 50 : 15 in simplest form?

   A. 10 : 3

   B. 3 : 10

   C. 25 : 3

   D. 5 : 3

SHOW YOUR WORK

$\dfrac{50}{15} \qquad \dfrac{10}{3}$

4. Which ratio is **36 : 72** in simplest form?

A. 2 : 3

B. 3 : 2

C. 1 : 2

D. 2 : 1

SHOW YOUR WORK

$$\frac{36}{72} = \frac{2}{4} = \frac{1}{2}$$

5. If $\frac{3}{4}$ of a gallon of paint covers $\frac{2}{3}$ of a wall, how much paint will be required to paint all 4 walls of a room?

A. 4 gallons

B. 4.5 gallons

C. 6 gallons

D. 7 gallons

SHOW YOUR WORK

$0.75 \times 0.666 = 1.5$

$1.2 \times 4 = 4.5$

6. Juan walks $1\frac{1}{4}$ miles to school every day. It takes him $\frac{1}{2}$ hour. If he walks the same pace after school, how long does it take him to walk $\frac{1}{4}$ mile?

A. 3 minutes

B. 4 minutes

C. 5 minutes

D. 6 minutes

SHOW YOUR WORK

hours per mile

$.50 \div 1.25 = 0.4$ hours

$0.4 \times 0.25 = 0.1$

$0.1 = 6$ minutes

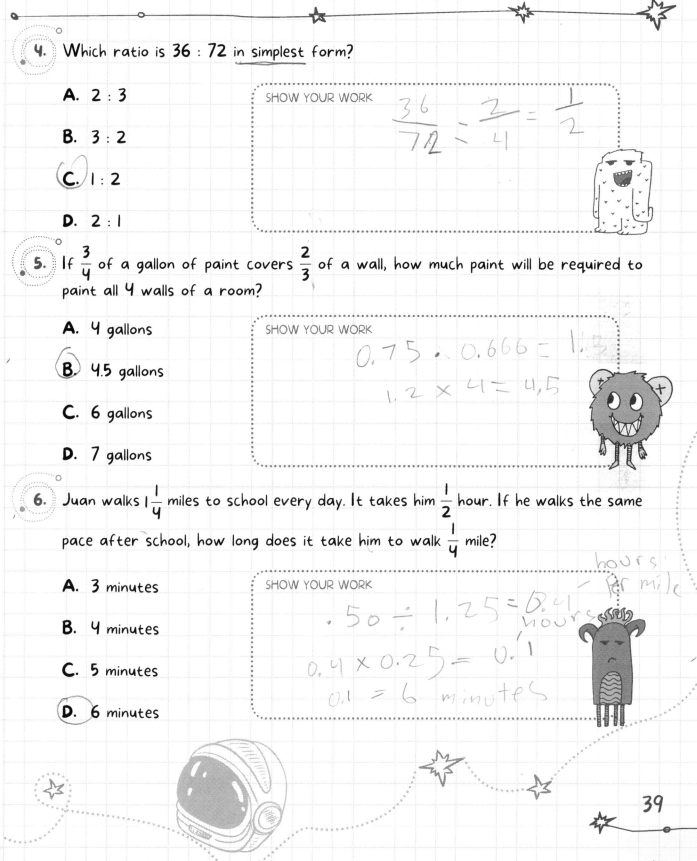

7. Which answer would be a correct value for *x* in the equation $y = 9x$ if $y = 72$?

A. 6

B. 7

C. 8

D. 9

SHOW YOUR WORK

$9 \times 8 = 72$

$x = 72$

8. Which answer would be a correct value for *y* in the equation $y = 3x$ if $x = 11$?

A. 30

B. 33

C. 36

D. 39

SHOW YOUR WORK

33

9. What is the constant rate for these values?

(1, 6) (4, 24) (8, 48)

A. 2

B. 4

C. 6

D. 8

SHOW YOUR WORK

6

10. What is the constant rate for these values?

x	y
3	12
6	24
9	36

SHOW YOUR WORK

A. 1   **B.** 2   **C.** 3   **D.** 4

11. If the relationship is represented by the equation $y = 10x$, and $y = 70$, what is x?

A. 6

B. 7

C. 8

D. 9

SHOW YOUR WORK

12. If you were to graph the line $y = 7x$, which point would fall on the line?

A. (0,0)

B. (1, 14)

C. (2, 7)

D. (3, 14)

SHOW YOUR WORK

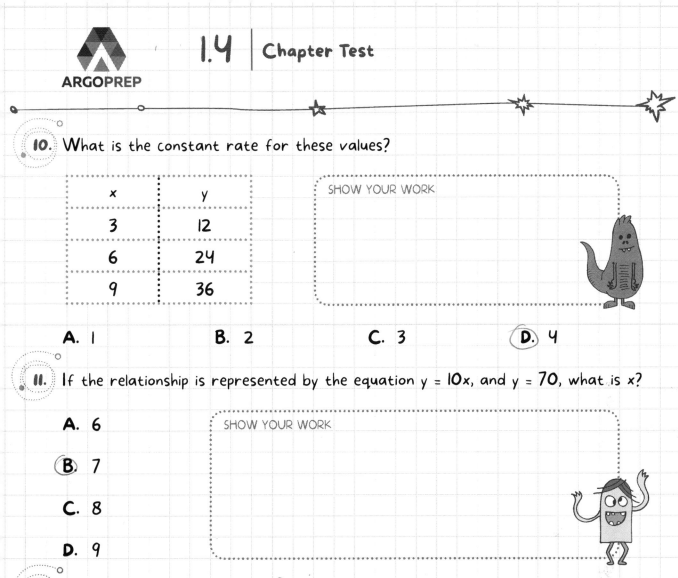

ARGOPREP

13. If you were to graph the line y = 2x, which point would fall on the line?

X Y

A. (10, 5)

SHOW YOUR WORK

B. (3, 2)

C. (2, 6)

D. (2, 4)

14. If you were to graph the line y = 4x, which point would fall on the line?

X Y

A. (6, 3)

SHOW YOUR WORK

B. (8, 2)

C. (1, 4)

D. (4, 1)

15. How much money would be in an account that starts with $45 and earns 2% interest a year over 10 years?

A. $36

SHOW YOUR WORK

$\frac{45}{1} \times \frac{2}{100} \times \frac{10}{1} = 9$

$\frac{45}{9}$

B. $58

C. $50

D. $54

16. Sam buys **$36** worth of books. He has to pay **3%** tax on his purchase. He has **$40**. Does he have enough money to make his purchase? Explain your response.

SHOW YOUR WORK

36 $\dfrac{36}{1} \times \dfrac{3}{100}$ Yes

37.08 1.08   37.08

step 1

17. A store is having a sale and reduces its holiday items by 75%. Emily is interested in buying a decoration that was originally priced at $240. What is the new price of the item?

A. $300

B. $60

C. $180

D. $430

SHOW YOUR WORK

240
− 1 8 0
6 0

18. Alleigh and her mom go out to lunch and their bill is $28. If they want to tip their waitress the standard 15%, what will the total amount of their bill be?

A. $31

B. $32

C. $32.20

D. $33

SHOW YOUR WORK

$28 \times \dfrac{15}{100} = \$4.20$

28
4.20
32.20

ARGOPREP

19. The number of students in 7th grade went from 180 last year to 160 this year. What was the percent decrease?

A. 11%

B. 12%

C. 13%

D. 14%

SHOW YOUR WORK

$$180 - 160 = 20$$

$$\frac{20}{180} = 0.111$$

$$11\%$$

20. Melissa's doctor estimated her height at 5 feet. Her actual height was 5 feet, 3 inches. What was her doctor's percent error?

A. 3%

B. 4%

C. 5%

D. 6%

SHOW YOUR WORK

$$63 - 63 = 3$$

$$\frac{3}{63} = 0.0417$$

$$5\%$$

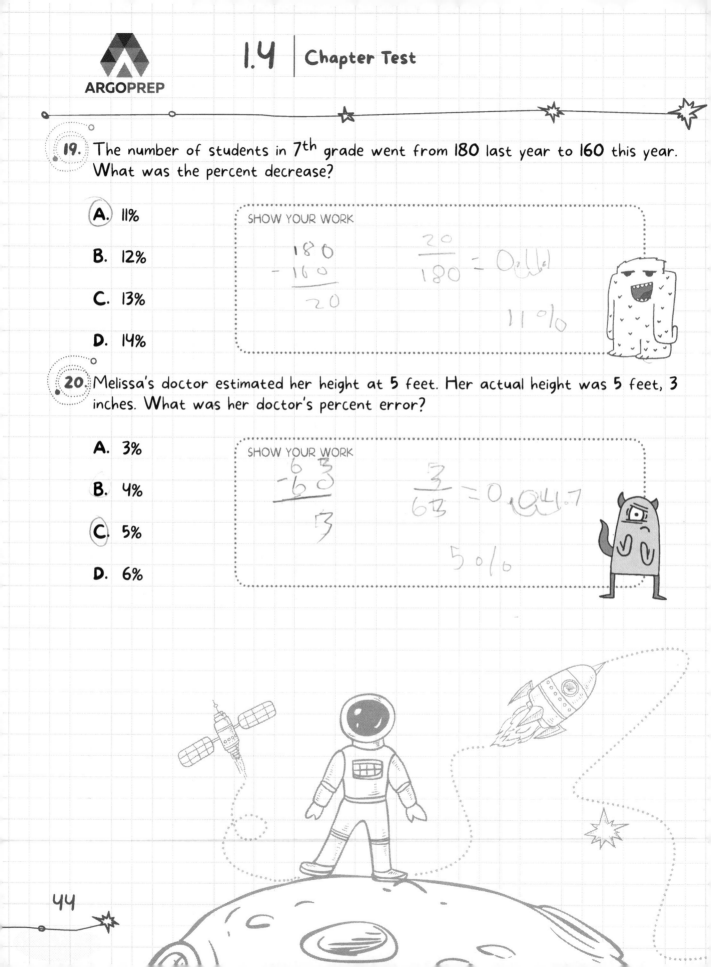

NOTES

NOT CORRECT ANSWER:

1) READ PROBLEM.
    - INFORMATION
    - WHAT IS ASKED FOR

2) FIX AN ERROR AT BEGINNING
    FIX ALL WAY THROUGH.

FOR SAT   Redo 13-20 - MIXED UP PROBLEMS

Next Session: SATURDAY 9:30

Chapter 2 :
The Number System

2.1. Apply and extend previous understandings of operations with fractions page 48

2.2. Apply and extend previous understandings of multiplication and division page 57

2.3. Solve real-world problems involving the four operations page 63

2.4. Chapter Test page 70

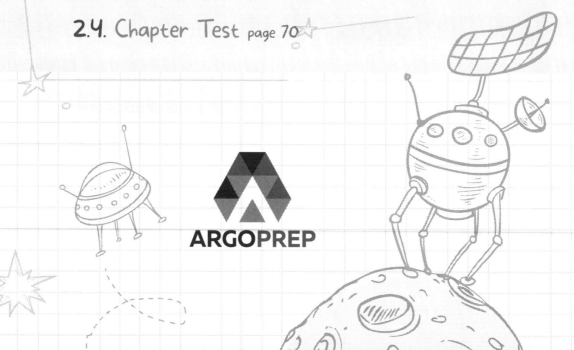

ARGOPREP

Let's review some information about **positive** and **negative numbers**. When we speak of positive and negative number operations, we are generally referring to integers or whole numbers. **We can use a number line to represent positive and negative numbers**.

The value of an integer represents the distance from **0** on the number line. **The positive or negative sign of an integer represents whether the number is to the left or right of zero. In terms of value, the positive or negative sign represents whether the number is greater than (right) or less than (left) of zero.**

We can combine opposite integers to get a value of **0**.

Let's look at an example. $-4 + 4 = 0$.

When we start at negative **4** and add a value of **4**, we end up with **0**.

It works the opposite way too. $4 + -4 = 0$.

When we start at positive **4** and add a value of **-4**, we end up with **0**.

We can apply what we know about numbers and their opposites to add and subtract positive and negative numbers.

You have been adding positive numbers since you were young. When you combine two numbers with a positive sign, you simply add the value of the numbers and keep the positive sign.

Review: 5 + 4 = 9

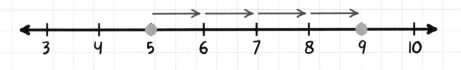

Adding two negative numbers is similar to adding two positive numbers. When you add two negative numbers, you combine their value and then carry the negative sign. This happens because when you are combining two negative numbers, their absolute value or distance from zero is growing.

Review: **-3** + -4 = -7

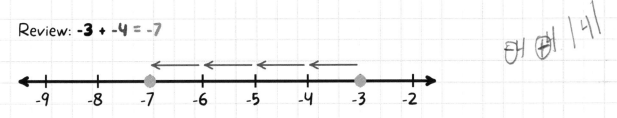

Adding a positive and negative number is a little more complicated. The first addend shows you where you start on the number line. Then you add the value of the second addend. If the second addend is positive, you move to the right on the number line or add the value. If the second addend is negative, you move to the left on the number line or subtract the value.

Review:

-6 + 8 =

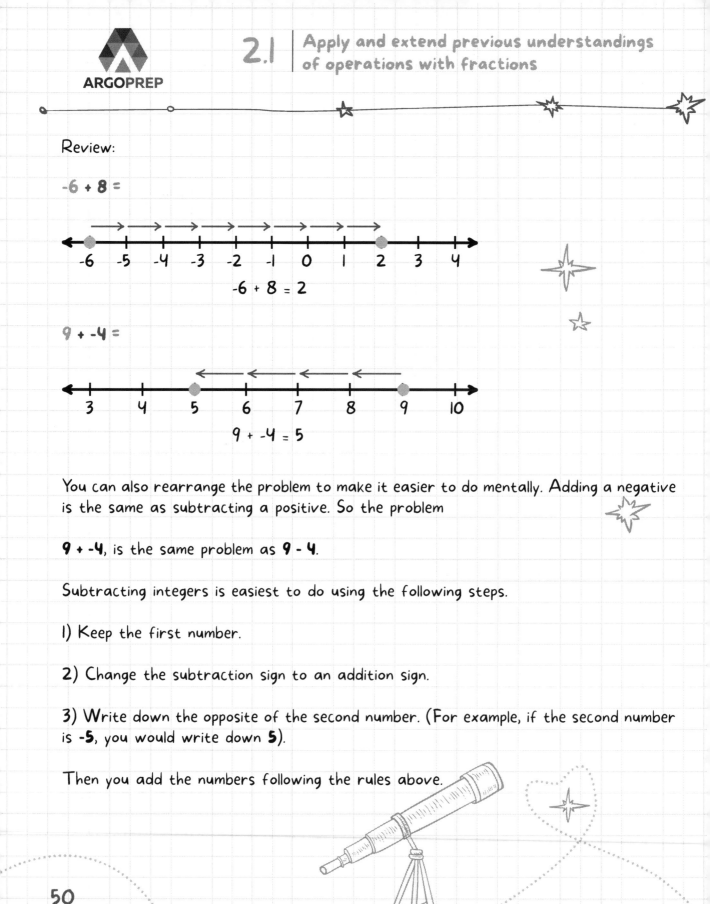

-6 + 8 = 2

9 + -4 =

9 + -4 = 5

You can also rearrange the problem to make it easier to do mentally. Adding a negative is the same as subtracting a positive. So the problem

9 + -4, is the same problem as **9 - 4**.

Subtracting integers is easiest to do using the following steps.

1) Keep the first number.

2) Change the subtraction sign to an addition sign.

3) Write down the opposite of the second number. (For example, if the second number is **-5**, you would write down **5**).

Then you add the numbers following the rules above.

Let's look at a few examples.

-5 - 6

Keep: **-5**
Change: **+**
Opposite: **-6**
Add: -5 + -6 = -11

9 - -5

Keep: **9**
Change: **+**
Opposite: **5**
Add: 9 + 5 = 14

-4 - -6

Keep: **-4**
Change: **+**
Opposite: **6**
Add: -4 + 6 = 2

NOTES

1. Which number can be added to 8 to get a sum of 0?

   A. -4

   B. 4

   C. -8

   D. 8

   SHOW YOUR WORK

2. Which number can be added to -11 to get a sum of 0?

   A. -11

   B. 11

   C. -5

   D. -6

   SHOW YOUR WORK

3. Which number can be subtracted from -23 to get a difference of 0?

   A. 23

   B. -23

   C. 67

   D. -67

   SHOW YOUR WORK

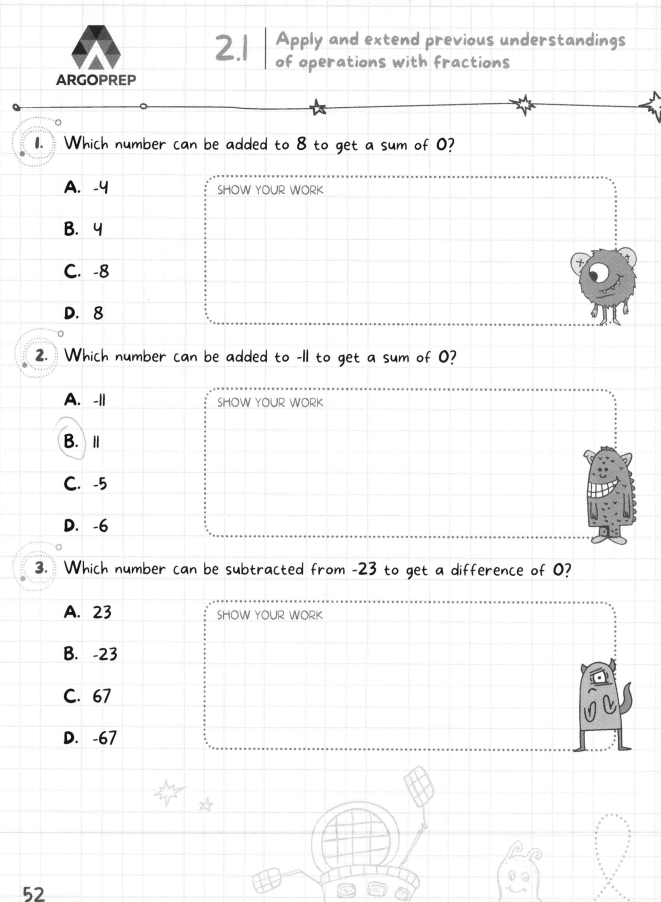

4. Which number can be subtracted from **38** to get a difference of **0**?

A. -83

B. 83

C. -38

D. 38

SHOW YOUR WORK

5. -23 + 37

A. -14

B. 14

C. 60

D. -60

SHOW YOUR WORK

6. -18 - 11

A. -7

B. 7

C. 29

D. -29

SHOW YOUR WORK

7. 32 + - 12

    A. -44

    B. 44

    C. 20

    D. -20

SHOW YOUR WORK

8. 68 - 89

    A. -21

    B. 21

    C. 42

    D. -42

SHOW YOUR WORK

9. 17 - -24

    A. 7

    B. -41

    C. 41

    D. 24

SHOW YOUR WORK

ARGOPREP

10. -17 + -21

A. 38

B. -38

C. 4

D. -4

SHOW YOUR WORK

11. -25 - -8

A. 17

B. -17

C. 32

D. -33

SHOW YOUR WORK

-25 + 8 = -17

12. 46 + -21

A. -67

B. 67

C. -25

D. 25

SHOW YOUR WORK

55

13. The highway speed limit had a posted speed of **65** mph. A driver was pulled over for going 13 mph over the speed limit. What was the driver's speed?

A. 78 mph

SHOW YOUR WORK

B. 52 mph

C. -52 mph

D. -13 mph

14. Michelle took her baby to the doctor. She was diagnosed as being **4** pounds underweight. If her original weight was **16** pounds, what was her weight when she was in the doctor's office?

A. 18 pounds

SHOW YOUR WORK

B. 16 pounds

C. 12 pounds

D. 20 pounds

15. My dad loves to golf. At his best round, he scored **2** under par. If he played **9** holes, which problem represents his potential scores?

A. 1 + 0 + -1 + -1 + 1 + 3 + 2 + -2 + -1

SHOW YOUR WORK

B. 2 + -1 + -1 + 1 + 0 + -2 +2 + -1+ -2

C. -2+ 1 + -1 + -1 + 0 + -2 +2 + -1 + -1

D. -1 + 0 + -2 + 2 + 1 + 3 + 2 + -2 + -1

We can apply our knowledge of multiplication and division to multiplying and dividing integers! When we multiply and divide integers, it is easiest to complete the operation first, multiply or divide, and then figure out the sign based on the rules below.

Let's start with two integers with the same sign. **When we multiply or divide two integers with the same sign, we end up with a positive result.**

A positive integer **x** a positive integer = a positive integer

Similarly, **a negative integer x a negative integer** = a positive integer

This is because when we multiply two negatives the negatives cancel each other out. This is also true when we have an even number of factors. **When we multiply four or six or eight or more negatives, we will always end up with a positive result as long as we have an even number of factors.**

When we multiply two integers with a different sign or an odd amount of negative integers, we end up with a negative result.

A positive integer **x** a negative integer = a negative integer

This works if you have three negative integers, or five, or seven, etc.

Integers are rational numbers. **A rational number is any number that can be expressed as a fraction made of two integers.** Because of this, when we have rational numbers that are decimals, that are consider rational numbers only if the decimal terminates (or ends at some point) or repeats. **If the decimal does not terminate or repeat, then the number is considered irrational.**

1. How does multiplying a factor by -1 change its value?

A. It makes the number negative.

B. It makes the number positive.

C. It makes the number equal to 0.

D. It depends on the sign of the factor.

SHOW YOUR WORK

2. Which example correct?

A. pos x neg = neg

B. neg x neg = neg

C. pos x pos x neg = pos

D. pos x neg x neg = neg

SHOW YOUR WORK

3. Which is incorrect?

A. pos x pos = neg

B. neg x pos = neg

C. neg x neg = pos

D. pos x neg x pos = neg

SHOW YOUR WORK

4. -4 x 15 =

A. -45

B. 45

C. -60

D. 60

SHOW YOUR WORK

5. -6 x -20 =

A. -12

B. 12

C. -120

D. 120

SHOW YOUR WORK

6. -75 ÷ 5 =

A. -15

B. 15

C. -13

D. 13

SHOW YOUR WORK

7. 108 ÷ -2 =

A. -54

B. 54

C. -52

D. 52

SHOW YOUR WORK

8. 16 × -5 =

A. 80

B. -80

C. 85

D. -85

SHOW YOUR WORK

9. -120 ÷ -6 =

A. -2

B. 2

C. 20

D. -20

SHOW YOUR WORK

10. -15 × -6 =

A. -80

B. 80

C. 90

D. -90

SHOW YOUR WORK

11. 12 × -8 =

A. -96

B. 96

C. -94

D. 94

SHOW YOUR WORK

12. The coldest day of the winter last year was -13°F. This year, the coldest day was three times as cold. What is the temperature this year?

A. -24°F

B. -39°F

C. -26°F

D. 39°F

SHOW YOUR WORK

$$\begin{array}{r} 13 \\ \times\ \ 3 \\ \hline 9 \end{array}$$

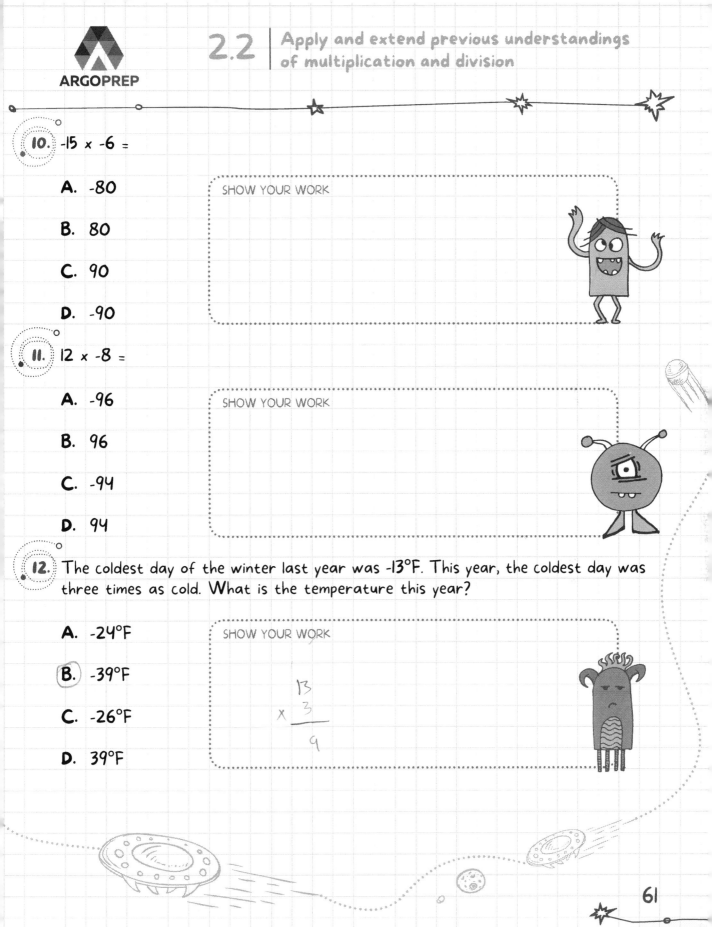

13. A submarine can dive at a rate of -120 feet per minute. Using the formula d=rt, how long will it take to reach **-3600** feet?

A. -3 minutes

B. -30 minutes

C. 3 minutes

D. 30 minutes

SHOW YOUR WORK

14. Which decimal represents a rational number?

A. 0.28197183128...

B. 0.2376428364...

C. 0.125125125...

D. 0.0298829702...

SHOW YOUR WORK

15. Which is an irrational number?

A. $\dfrac{1}{3}$

B. .713465...

C. $\dfrac{1}{6}$

D. $\dfrac{2}{5}$

SHOW YOUR WORK

We can use our knowledge to solve word problems involving integers. A few pointers to keep in mind:

1) When you read a word problem involving integers, **first you need to identify whether the numbers involved in the problem are positive or negative**. You need to carefully think about the situation mentioned and then **determine which values are appropriate**.

2) Next, you need to figure out **which operation is involved in solving the problem**.

3) You use the information you have gathered from 1 and 2 to create a problem.

4) You complete your work!

5) Check your answer. Review the label and be sure your answer makes sense in terms of the real world situation.

Let's see an example:

1) When you read a word problem involving integers, first you need to identify whether the numbers involved in the problem are positive or negative. You need to carefully think about the situation mentioned and then determine which valuare appropriate.

Ed owes his father $86. If he every month he reduces his debt by $6 a week, how many weeks will it take to pay back his dad?

Ed owes -86.

The debt reduces -6 a week.

The number of weeks should be positive.

2) Next, you need to figure out which operation is involved in solving the problem.

To solve this problem, you should divide the amount owed by the amount of money paid per week.

3) You use the information you have gathered from 1 and 2 to create a problem.

$$-86 \div -6 = ?$$

4) You complete your work!

$$-86 \div -6 = 14\frac{1}{3}$$

5) Check your answer. Review the label and be sure your answer makes sense in terms of the real world situation.

$-86 \div -6 = 14\frac{1}{3}$, so it would take **15 weeks** to pay his dad back.

 1. The city of New Orleans is located at **8** feet below sea level. the highest point in Louisiana is Driskill Mountain is **535** feet above sea level. If Elizabeth travels from New Orleans to Driskill Mountain, what is her change in elevation?

A. 543 ft

B. 527 ft

C. 551 ft

D. 519 ft

SHOW YOUR WORK

2. The lowest point in the United States is Death Valley, which has an elevation of **282** feet below sea level. The highest point in California is Mt Whitney, which has an elevation of **14,494** feet above sea level. How much higher is Mt Whitney than Death Valley?

A. -14212 feet

B. 13390 feet

C. 14212 feet

D. 14776 feet

SHOW YOUR WORK

14,494
282
―――――
14,776

3. Alejandro's mom works at Death Valley and drives there every day for work. If she drives eight times a week from their house, which is at sea level, and the elevation is **-282** feet below sea level, what is the total elevation change she drives each week?

A. -275 feet

B. -290 feet

C. -2256 feet

D. 2256 feet

SHOW YOUR WORK

-282
x

-282
8
x

4. The lowest point in France is **33** feet below sea level. The lowest point in Denmark is **23** feet below sea level. How much lower is the lowest point in France?

A. 10 feet

B. -10 feet

C. 56 feet

D. -56 feet

SHOW YOUR WORK

5. The Dead Sea has an elevation of **-1404** feet. Mount Meron has an elevation of **3,963** feet. What is the different in elevation?

A. 5,367 feet

B. -5,367 feet

C. 2,559 feet

D. -2,559 feet

SHOW YOUR WORK

6. Bryan withdraws $215 from his bank account to buy a game system. He earns $15 a yard mowing lawns and tries to mow four lawns a week. How long would he take to earn his saved money back?

A. 1 week

B. 2 weeks

C. 3 weeks

D. 4 weeks

SHOW YOUR WORK

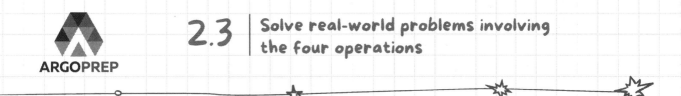
7. Temperatures in Alaska for four months are -14°F, -11°F, -6°F, and -2°F. What is the average temperature for these four months?

A. -8°F

B. 7.75°F

C. -8.25°F

D. 8.25°F

SHOW YOUR WORK

8. Temperatures in Alaska for four months are 56°F, -2°F, -7°F and 32°F. What is the average temperature for these four months?

A. 19.75°F

B. -19.75°F

C. 9.75°F

D. -8.75°F

SHOW YOUR WORK

23 2
- 9
23
56
79

9. Mr. Wilkes deducts **5** points out of **100** for every misspelled word on a final draft. Joe misspelled six words on his draft. What was his final score?

A. 95

B. 70

C. 105

D. 75

SHOW YOUR WORK

10. Temperatures in Alaska for four months are -3°F, -12°F, -6°F and 4°F. What is the average temperature over those four months?

A. 7°F

B. -7°F

C. 17°F

D. -4.25°F

SHOW YOUR WORK

11. Last week it was twice as cold as it was this week. If it is -6°F this week, what was the temperature last week?

A. 6°F

B. 12°F

C. 0°F

D. -12°F

SHOW YOUR WORK

12. Mount Everest is **29,028** feet above sea level. If a climber has climbed Everest three times, how high above sea level has he gone?

A. 87,084

B. 88,074

C. 84,870

D. 87,804

SHOW YOUR WORK

13. Which problem could represent 15 degrees below normal temperature?

A. 0-5

B. 0-15

C. 5-0

D. 15-0

SHOW YOUR WORK

14. Which problem could represent that a team scored 36 fewer points last year?

A. 12-24

B. 24-24

C. 45-36

D. 36-15

SHOW YOUR WORK

15. Which problem could represent an increase in height of 13 inches?

A. 0-13

B. 53-13

C. 63-13

D. 63+13

SHOW YOUR WORK

1. Which number can be added to -73 to make a sum of 0?

A. 73

B. -73

C. 34

D. -34

SHOW YOUR WORK

2. 42 + -36

A. -78

B. 78

C. 6

D. -6

SHOW YOUR WORK

3. -22 - 37

A. 15

B. -15

C. 59

D. -59

SHOW YOUR WORK

4. 78 - 25

A. -53

B. 53

C. 93

D. 103

SHOW YOUR WORK

5. -56 + -23

A. -79

B. 79

C. -23

D. 23

SHOW YOUR WORK

6. -43 - -38

A. 86

B. -86

C. -5

D. -10

SHOW YOUR WORK

ARGOPREP

7. -73 + -27

A. 100

B. 46

C. -46

D. -100

SHOW YOUR WORK

8. -47 - 26

A. 73

B. -73

C. -21

D. 21

SHOW YOUR WORK

9. -6 x -15

A. 90

B. -90

C. 95

D. -95

SHOW YOUR WORK

10. 92 ÷ -4

A. -24

B. -22

C. 24

D. -23

SHOW YOUR WORK

11. -4 × 17

A. 64

B. -64

C. -68

D. 68

SHOW YOUR WORK

12. -105 ÷ 5

A. 21

B. -21

C. 22

D. -22

SHOW YOUR WORK

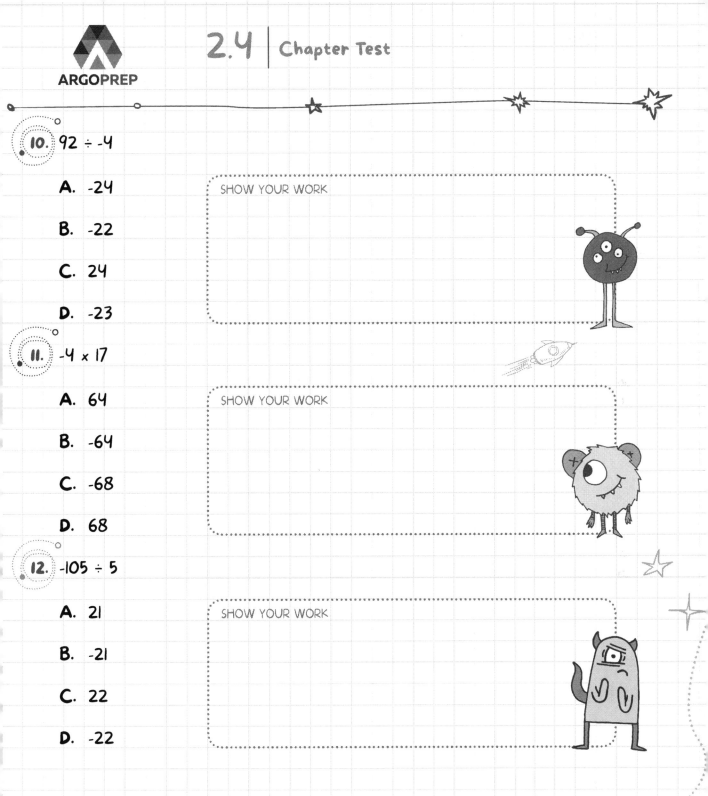

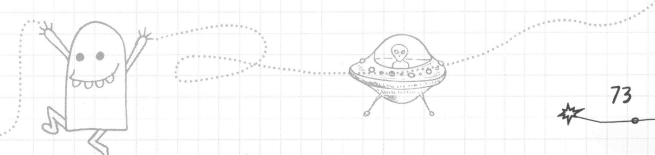

13. 7 x 13

A. -91

B. 91

C. 92

D. -92

SHOW YOUR WORK

14. 14 x -6

A. -84

B. 84

C. -80

D. 80

SHOW YOUR WORK

15. -186 ÷ -3

A. -64

B. 64

C. -62

D. 62

SHOW YOUR WORK

16. John likes to golf. His best score is **-3**. Which problem could represent his round?

A. -1 + 2 - 1 - 1 - 1 + 0 - 1 + 2 - 1

B. -1 + 1 - 1 - 1 - 1 + 0 - 1 + 1 - 1

C. -2 + 3 - 1 - 1 - 2 + 0 - 1 + 2 - 1

D. 1 + 1 + 1

SHOW YOUR WORK

17. Four months in Alaska have the following temperatures: -15°C, -11°C, 4°C, 2°C. What is the average temperature for those four months?

A. -2°C

B. 2°C

C. -5°C

D. 4°C

SHOW YOUR WORK

18. The average surface temperature on a few planets are as follows: -162°F, -10°F and -81°F. What is the average surface temperature for these three planets?

A. -84.3°F

B. 84°F

C. -83°F

D. 83°F

SHOW YOUR WORK

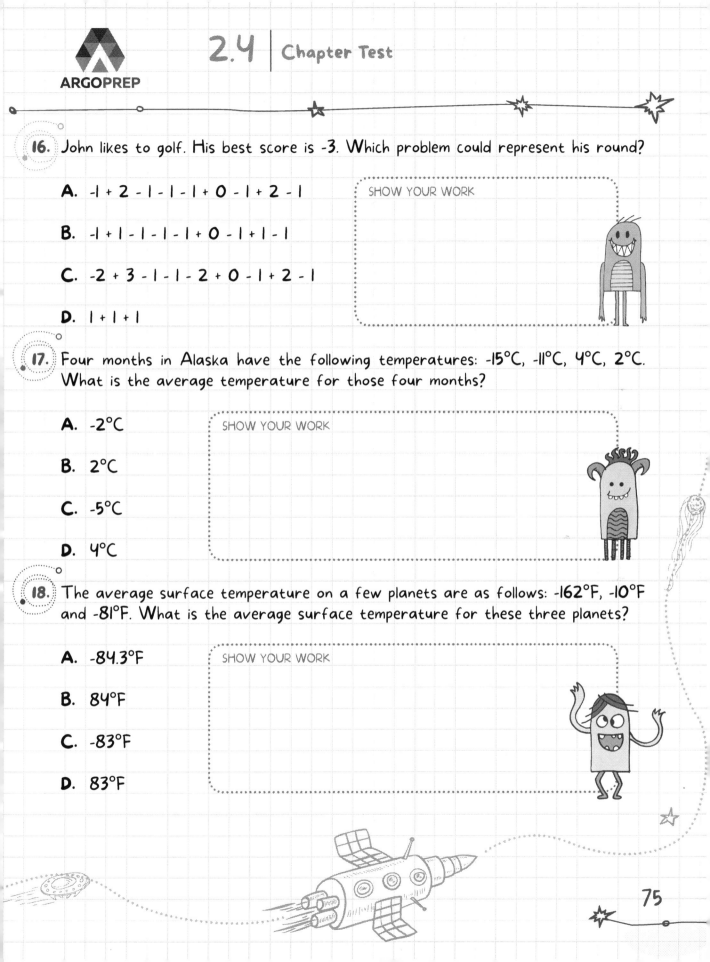

19. Marisa pays **$20** a month in her cell phone. If she has **$320** in her account, how long will she be able to pay for her cell phone before she runs out of money?

A. 13 months

B. 10 months

C. 6 months

D. 16 months

SHOW YOUR WORK

20. The highest part in the Netherlands is **2,910** feet above sea level. The lowest part is **22** feet below sea level. If we drive from the highest to lowest part, what is the total elevation we cover?

A. 2,088 feet

B. 2,080 feet

C. 2,932 feet

D. 2,880 feet

SHOW YOUR WORK

ARGOPREP

NOTES

Chapter 3 :
Expressions and Equations

3.1. Use properties of operations to generate equivalent expressions. page 80

3.2. Solve real-life and mathematical problems using numerical and algebraic expressions and equations. page 98

3.3. Chapter Test page 116

ARGOPREP

We can use the operation rules we reviewed in the last chapter to combine like expressions. First, let's review a few terms.

A variable is an unknown quantity represented by a letter, usually x

Variables often are accompanied by coefficients, which are integers that perform some operation with the variable. $4x$ or $2y$

An expression can be made up of terms, which can be numbers, variables or a product of a combination of numbers and variables. $4x + 3$

We can simplify expressions by combining like terms. We do this to make the expression easier to solve or evaluate. Let's look at an example.

$4x + 3x + 2 - 6 + 2y$

First, we need to determine, what terms are similar and can be combined.

In this expression, we have **3** different terms.

$4x, 3x$

$+2, -6$

$2y$

We use our knowledge of operations to combine the coefficients of the variables for $4x + 3x$.

$4 + 3 = 7$, so the variable and coefficient can be simplified to $7x$

We use our knowledge of operations to combine $+2$ and -6.

$+2 - 6 = -4$

$2y$ is already in simpliest form.

So, $4x + 3x + 2 - 6 + 2y = 7x - 4 + 2y$

Usually, we put all the variables with coefficients and then the number, so

$7x + 2y - 4$

We can also use our knowledge of the distributive property to factor and expand expressions. **When we factor an expression, we determine what factor is similar to each term and remove it.**

Let's look at an example: $5m + 10n - 60$

What is the greatest common factor of 5, 10 and 60? **5**

If we divide each term by **5**, what do we have left? **1, 2 and 12**

We then express the factor using parentheses to represent the distributive property.

5(m + 2n - 12)

Pay close attention to your positive and negative signs when you complete these problems!

We can reverse those steps to expand expressions.

Let's look at another example: **3(2f - 6g)**

We take **3 × 2** and then **3 × -6**

Our answer becomes 6f - 18g.

1. Simplify. 4a + 6a -2b +8b -5

   A. 16a - 5

   B. 11a

   C. 10a - b

   D. 10a + 6b - 5

SHOW YOUR WORK

2. Simplify. 8y - 3y + 4 - 8

   A. 11y + 12

   B. y

   C. 5y - 4

   D. 4y - 5

SHOW YOUR WORK

$5y - 8 + 4$

3. Simplify. 8d - 5 - 2 + 4b

   A. 4d - 8b

   B. 8d + 4b - 7

   C. d + 4b

   D. 5b

SHOW YOUR WORK

4. Simplify. $10x - 3y + 8x - 7y$

   A. $10x - 18y$

   B. $10xy$

   C. $28xy$

   D. $18x - 10y$

SHOW YOUR WORK

5. Simplify. $5g + 4h - 6 + 2$

   A. $5g + 4h - 4$

   B. $5g$

   C. $5g + 4h$

   D. $9g$

SHOW YOUR WORK

6. Simplify. $7h - 2y + 6y$

   A. $7h + 4y$

   B. $11h$

   C. $7h - 4y$

   D. $4h - 7y$

SHOW YOUR WORK

7. Factor. $49x + 63y$

   A. $7x + 9y$

   B. $7(7x + 9y)$

   C. $7(9x + 7y)$

   D. $9x + 7y$

SHOW YOUR WORK

8. Factor. $16a - 4$

   A. $a - 1$

   B. $4(4a + 1)$

   C. $4(4a - 1)$

   D. $4(4a)$

SHOW YOUR WORK

9. Factor. $18x + 14y - 20$

   A. $2(9x + 7y - 10)$

   B. $2(7x + 9y + 10)$

   C. $9x + 7y - 10$

   D. $2(9x + 7y)$

SHOW YOUR WORK

10. Factor. 54m - 81n - 9

A. 9(4m - 3n)

B. 9(-6m - 9n - 1)

C. 9(-6m + 9n + 1)

D. -9(-6m + 9n + 1)

SHOW YOUR WORK

11. Factor. 8k - 4y + 2

A. 4(2k + 1)

B. 8(k - 1)

C. 2(4k - 2y + 1)

D. 4(2k - 1)

SHOW YOUR WORK

12. Factor. 81b + 27c - 15d

A. 9(73b + 18c - 6d)

B. 3(27b + 9c - 5d)

C. 9(9b + 3c - 15d)

D. 6(24b + 4c - 3d)

SHOW YOUR WORK

$$3(27b + 4c - 5d)$$

13. Factor. $35 - 40y$

    A. $5(7 - 8y)$

    B. $7(5 - 8y)$

    C. $5(-7 - 8y)$

    D. $5(7 + 8y)$

SHOW YOUR WORK

$$7(5 - 8y)$$
$$35 - 40y$$

14. Distribute. $3(2y - 6x + 2)$

    A. $5y - 9x + 5$

    B. $6y + 18x - 6$

    C. $6y - 18x + 6$

    D. $18y - 6x + 6$

SHOW YOUR WORK

$$3(2y - 6x + 2)$$
$$(6y - 18x + 6)$$

15. Distribute. $2(b + c + d)$

    A. $2bcd$

    B. $2b + 2c + 2d$

    C. $2 + b + c + d$

    D. $2bc + 2dc$

SHOW YOUR WORK

16. Distribute. $4(6n - 5m)$

A. $2n - m$

B. $10n + 9m$

C. $24m - 20n$

D. $24n - 20m$

SHOW YOUR WORK

$4(6n - 5m)$

$(24n - 20m)$

17. Distribute. $10(-x - 10y)$

A. $-100x - 10y$

B. $-10x - 10y$

C. $-10x - 100y$

D. $10x - 100y$

SHOW YOUR WORK

$10x - x = -10x$

$10x - 10y = -100y$

$-10x - 100y$

18. Distribute. $-8(y - 2)$

A. $-8y + 16$

B. $-8y - 16$

C. $8y - 16$

D. $8y + 16$

SHOW YOUR WORK

87

19. Distribute. $-5(3a - 4b + c)$

A. $15a - 20b + 5c$

B. $-15a + 20b - 5c$

C. $-15a - 20b + 5c$

D. $15a + 20b - 5c$

SHOW YOUR WORK

$-5(3a - 4b + c)$
$-15a + 20 + 5c$

20. Distribute. $12b (4 + 6)$

A. $60b$

B. $72b$

C. $48b$

D. $120b$

SHOW YOUR WORK

NOTES

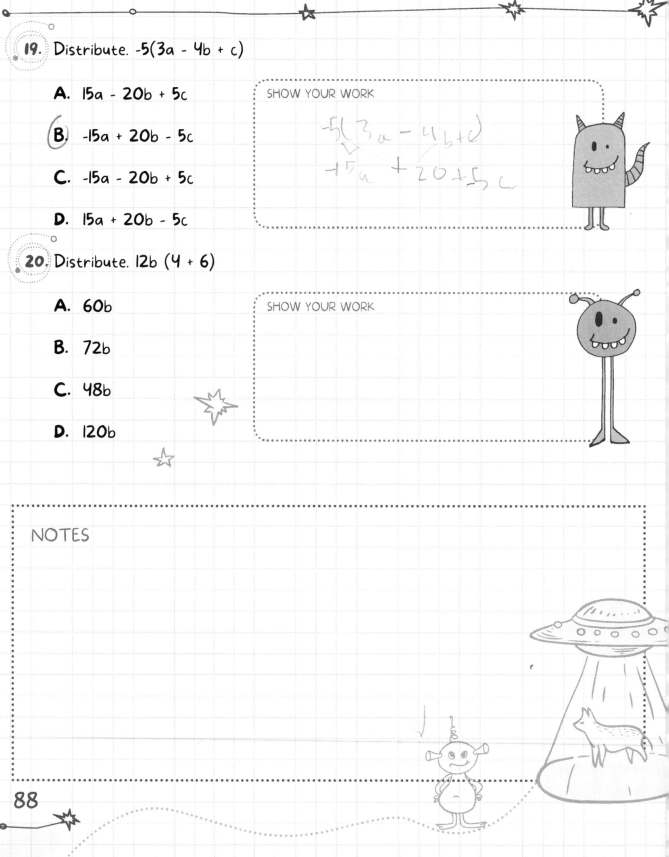

Linear expressions expressed as numbers and operations can also be expressed as words. For example, if you have the linear expression

a + 3

You can express that as **three more than an unknown quantity**, a.

We can apply our understanding of linear expressions to real world situations. This is helpful because translating word problems into linear expressions can help us solve word problems easier. When changing a word problem into a linear expression, you should follow these steps:

First - determine the unknown quantity and set it up as a variable.

Second - determine how the unknown quantity relates to the quantities given in the problem.

Third - combine the quantities and variables in a way that makes sense in the problem. Let's look at an example.

Ed is at a library. He enters with 20 books. He returns some of the books.

What do we not know in this situation? We do not know how many books Ed returns.

So x = **the number of books Ed returns.**

What quantity do we know? We know Ed enters the library with 20 books.

How do we combine the quantities?

If Ed starts with 20 books and returns some, we should subtract the unknown quantity from the known quantity. So the expression will be:

20 - x

1. Five less than a variable y

A. 1 - y - 5

B. y + 5

C. 5 - y

D. y - 5

SHOW YOUR WORK

2. Six more than a variable b

A. b - 6

B. b + 6

C. 6 - b

D. 6b

SHOW YOUR WORK

B + 6

3. The product of a variable x and seven

A. x - 7

B. 7 - x

C. 7x

D. 7 + x

SHOW YOUR WORK

3.1.B | Use properties of operations to generate equivalent expressions

4. Eight less than double a variable n

A. 2n - 8

B. 16 - n

C. 8n - 2

D. 16n

SHOW YOUR WORK

2n - 8

5. The product of a variable and eleven

A. 11a

B. 11 + a

C. 11 - a

D. $\frac{11}{a}$

SHOW YOUR WORK

11 × a = 11a

6. 10 more than 5 times a variable d

A. 10d + 5

B. 5d + 10

C. 50d

D. $\frac{d}{50}$

SHOW YOUR WORK

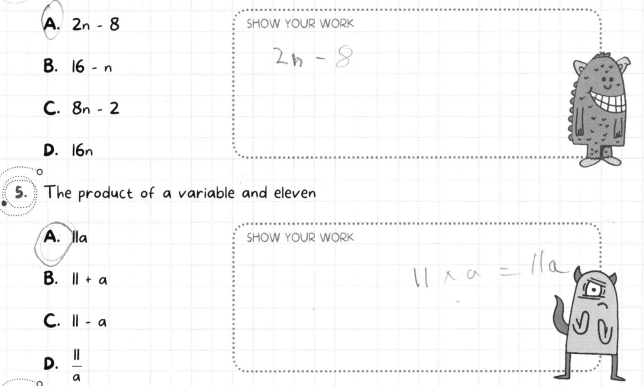

7. Fifteen less than a variable c

A. 15c

B. 15 - c

C. c - 15

D. $\frac{15}{c}$

SHOW YOUR WORK

8. Nine more than a product of three and a variable h

A. $\frac{h}{27}$

B. 27h

C. 9h + 3

D. 3h + 9

SHOW YOUR WORK

3h + 9

9. A variable t divided by 8

A. $\frac{8}{t}$

B. $\frac{t}{8}$

C. 8t

D. 8 - t

SHOW YOUR WORK

10. 10 more than a number

A. 10 - n

SHOW YOUR WORK

B. n - 10

C. 10 + n

D. 10n

11. A variable x divided by 2 and then increased by 11

A. 11x + 2

SHOW YOUR WORK

B. 2x + 11

C. $\frac{2}{x} + 11$

D. $\frac{x}{2} + 11$

12. 3x - 7

A. Seven less than a variable x tripled

B. variable times seven minus three

C. Three less than seven times a variable

D. Three less than the product of three and a variable

SHOW YOUR WORK

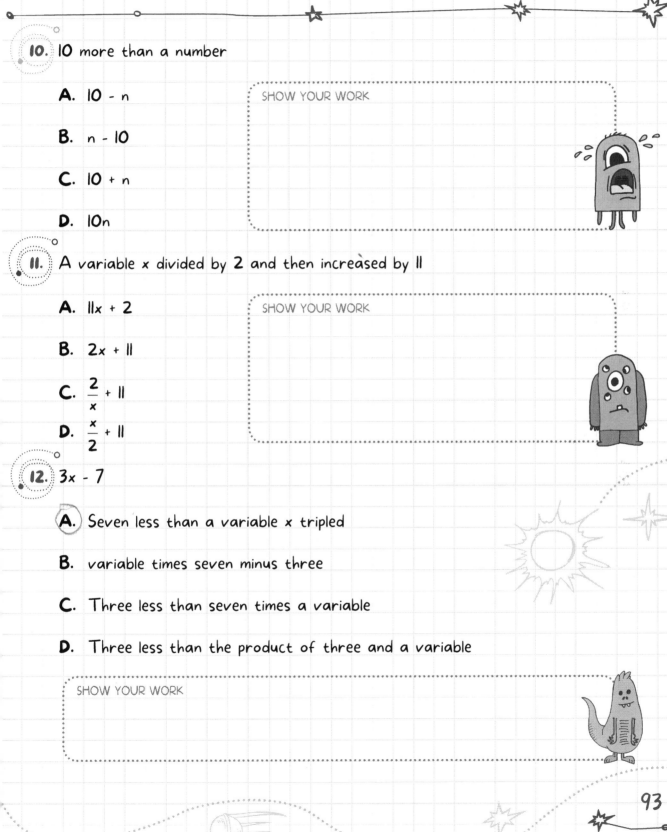

13. 14d

A. Fourteen less than a variable

B. The product of fourteen and a variable d

C. A variable divided by 14

D. Fourteen more than a variable

SHOW YOUR WORK

14. a + 4

A. Four less than a variable a

B. Four more than a variable x

C. Four more than a variable a

D. Four less than a variable x

SHOW YOUR WORK

15. $\dfrac{5c}{3}$

A. The product of 5 and a variable tripled

B. Five more than a variable c divided by 3

C. The product of 3 and a variable minus five

D. The product of 5 and a variable c divided by 3

SHOW YOUR WORK

16. A garden has a length of 15. Write an expression that illustrates its perimeter.

A. 30 + 2w

B. 15 + w

C. 15 + 2w

D. 30 + w

SHOW YOUR WORK

15

w — w

15

30 + 2w

17. A garden has a length of 15. Write an expression that illustrates its area.

A. 15 + w

B. 30w

C. 15w

D. 30 + w

SHOW YOUR WORK

18. A garden has a width of 8. Write an expression that illustrates its area.

A. L + 8

B. 8L

C. 2L + 16

D. 2L

SHOW YOUR WORK

8 - [scribble] - 8

8.L

19. Sarah mows lawns for $24 per lawn. Write an expression that illustrates how much she earns in a week, if m = the number of lawns she mows.

A. 24 - m

B. m + 24

C. 24 + m

D. 24m

SHOW YOUR WORK

20. John earns an allowance of $12 a week. Write an expression that illustrates how much he earns over a longer period of time if w = the number of weeks he earns the allowance.

A. w - 12

B. 12 - w

C. 12w

D. 12 + w

SHOW YOUR WORK

12w

NOTES

What is a rational number? **Remember a rational number is a number that can be expressed as ratio or fraction. We can perform operations with rational numbers just as we perform operations with whole numbers and integers.** One key to success is rational numbers is that when performing operations, rational numbers need to be in the same form (percents should only be added to percents, for example).

So when performing operations, first be sure all numbers in the problem are in the same form.

Rational numbers follow order of operations.

Remember, order of operations is as follows:

Parenthesis, Exponents, Multiplication and Division (from left to right), Addition and Subtraction (from left to right).

Rational numbers also follow the rules of positive and negative integers.

We can use rational numbers to solve word problems. Let's look at an example.

Emily has **3** cats that each weigh $5\frac{3}{4}$ pounds. If one cat gained $\frac{1}{2}$ pound, one cat remained the same and one cat lost **0.25** pounds, how much was their new total weight?

First- we should determine all the numbers are in the appropriate form.

$3, 5\frac{3}{4}, \frac{1}{2}$, **0.25** are not. I will change **0.25** to $\frac{1}{4}$ so it matches the rest of the numbers in fraction form.

Now we write the problem:

The original weight of the cats is $3 \times 5\frac{3}{4}$

One cat adds $\frac{1}{2}$, one cat stays the same and one cat subtracts $\frac{1}{4}$.

$$3 \times 5\frac{3}{4} + \frac{1}{2} - \frac{1}{4}$$

To solve, we follow order of operations:

$$3 \times 5\frac{3}{4} = \frac{3}{1} \times \frac{23}{4} = \frac{69}{4}$$

I will leave that as a mixed number so it is easy to use for addition and subtraction.

$$\frac{69}{4} + \frac{1}{2} - \frac{1}{4}$$

$$\frac{69}{4} + \frac{2}{4} - \frac{1}{4} =$$

$$\frac{70}{4} = 17\frac{2}{4} = 17\frac{1}{2} \text{ pounds}$$

Does this answer make sense?

Let's look at the problem again.

Emily has 3 cats that each weigh $5\frac{3}{4}$ pounds. If one cat gained $\frac{1}{2}$ pound, one cat remained the same and one cat lost 0.25 pounds, how much was their new total weight?

The cats start at $\frac{69}{4}$ pounds, which is $17\frac{1}{4}$ pounds. Their weight doesn't change that much, so the correct answer should be close to their original weight, which it is. Nice work!

1. $16\% \times 7.75 =$

A. 112.75

B. $25\frac{1}{3}$

C. $1\frac{2}{25}$

D. $1\frac{6}{25}$

SHOW YOUR WORK

2. $\frac{6}{9} + 3.1 =$

A. $18\frac{1}{9}$

B. $3\frac{6}{7}$

C. 3.76

D. 3.77

SHOW YOUR WORK

3. $14.77 \div -\frac{7}{8} =$

A. 16.88

B. -16.88

C. 12.25

D. -12.25

SHOW YOUR WORK

4. $-\dfrac{6}{10} + 3.3 =$

A. $2\dfrac{7}{10}$

B. $-5\dfrac{7}{10}$

C. $3\dfrac{9}{10}$

D. $-3\dfrac{9}{10}$

SHOW YOUR WORK

5. $\dfrac{1}{2}(3 + 2.1) =$

A. 10.2

B. -10.2

C. -2.55

D. 2.55

SHOW YOUR WORK

6. $3^2 - \left(4.2 \times \dfrac{3}{4}\right)$

A. -10.16

B. 10.16

C. -5.85

D. 5.85

SHOW YOUR WORK

7. $-4 \div 2 + 8.2 - (-5.1) =$

A. -1.55

B. 1.55

C. 11.3

D. -11.3

SHOW YOUR WORK

8. $-3 \times 6 \div -2 + (\frac{1}{2} - \frac{1}{6}) =$

A. $-9\frac{1}{3}$

B. $9\frac{1}{3}$

C. $27\frac{2}{3}$

D. $-27\frac{2}{3}$

SHOW YOUR WORK

9. Which choice is the same as 84%?

A. $\frac{21}{25}$

B. $\frac{22}{25}$

C. $\frac{48}{50}$

D. $\frac{84}{50}$

SHOW YOUR WORK

10. Which choice is the same as $6\frac{3}{5}$?

A. -12.6

B. 12.6

C. 6.6

D. -6.6

SHOW YOUR WORK

11. Which choice is the same as -4.68

A. 46.8%

B. 4.68%

C. $-4\frac{17}{25}$

D. $4\frac{17}{25}$

SHOW YOUR WORK

12. Which choice is the same as 39%?

A. 0.39

B. 3.9

C. 39.39

D. 3.09

SHOW YOUR WORK

13. Kristen ran a race that is 13.1 miles. Her average pace is 7 miles per hour. If she has completed $\frac{1}{2}$ of the race, approximately how long does she have to go?

A. 10 minutes

B. 6 hours

C. 6 minutes

D. 1 hour

SHOW YOUR WORK

14. We are baking cupcakes for a fundraiser. We have been asked to make 60 cupcakes, $\frac{3}{4}$ of them chocolate and the rest vanilla. If each chocolate cupcake will be $0.50 and each vanilla cupcake will be $0.75, how much will we make total from the sale?

A. $34.25

B. $33.75

C. $22.50

D. $2250

SHOW YOUR WORK

ARGOPREP

15. Robert deposited money in a bank account that earns **3%** simple interest every year. If he invests **$225** the first year, after three years, how much money will be in his bank account? Remember, the formula, interest = principal x rate x time.

A. $225

B. $231.75

C. $245.25

D. $252

SHOW YOUR WORK

16. John's exercise class has **32** people registered. $\frac{2}{3}$ of the people must arrive or he has to cancel class. If **60** people are in the gym and **45%** of them are planning to attend John's class, can he offer the class? Justify your answer by showing your work.

SHOW YOUR WORK

17. Which answer is a reasonable estimate for **15%** of **3.75**?

A. 0.5

B. 5

C. 50

D. 15

SHOW YOUR WORK

18. Which answer is a reasonable estimate for $-2.3 \times \frac{3}{8}$?

A. -1

B. 1

C. -2

D. 2

SHOW YOUR WORK

19. Which answer is a reasonable estimate for $16.8 + -\frac{2}{7}$?

A. 17

B. 16.5

C. 17.2

D. 23.2

SHOW YOUR WORK

20. Which answer is a reasonable estimate for $2(2.34 \times 2)$?

A. 4

B. 6

C. 8

D. 10

SHOW YOUR WORK

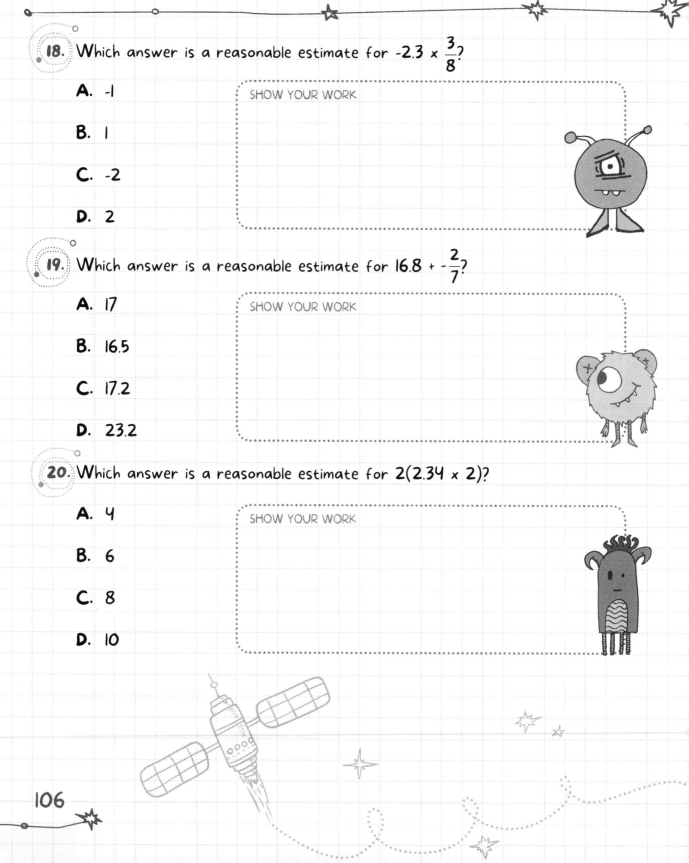

We can use our knowledge of operations and expressions to solve equations and inequalities.

Before we review how, let's look at a few terms related to equations and inequalities.

An equation is formed when we have to expressions equal to each other.

Remember **an expression can be a number, a variable or a combination or a number and a variable**.

To solve an equation, we **perform equal operations to each side with the goal of isolating the variable**. To determine which operation, we **work on reverse order of operations**.

Let's look at an example.

$x + 4 = 9$

We are adding 4 to the variable so to get the variable alone, we subtract 4 from both sides.

$$x + 4 = 9$$
$$ -4 \quad -4$$

$$x = 5$$

If the equation has multiple steps, you continue to do reverse order of operations until the variable is completely isolated.

Let's look at another example.

$3x - 5 = 16$

First, we add 5 to both sides. The equation becomes

$3x = 21$

Then, we divide 3 from each side.

When we do that, we get $x = 7$.

We solve inequalities in the same way that we solve equations.

The only difference is that when we multiply or divide an inequality by a negative number, we have to switch the sign from lesser than to greater than (or from greater than to lesser than).

Here's an example:

$n - 9 > 4$

To solve, you add 9 to both sides. Your answer would be $n > 13$.

Another example:

$\frac{n}{-2} + 4 < -8$

First, you subtract 4 from both sides.

The problem becomes $\frac{n}{-2} < -12$.

To isolate the n, you multiply both sides by -2. Because you are multiplying by a negative number, you also have to flip the sign.

The answer is $n > 24$.

We can set up word problems as equations or inequalities and then solve them to find the answer!

1. $2x - 13 = 9$

A. $x = 11$

B. $x = 2$

C. $x = 3$

D. $x = 15$

SHOW YOUR WORK

2. $x + 4 = 16$

A. $x = 4$

B. $x = 16$

C. $x = 20$

D. $x = 12$

SHOW YOUR WORK

3. $\frac{n}{5} = 12$

A. $n = 5$

B. $n = 17$

C. $n = 60$

D. $n = 12$

SHOW YOUR WORK

4. $y + 2 = -11$

A. $y = 13$

B. $y = -13$

C. $y = -9$

D. $y = 9$

SHOW YOUR WORK

5. $4m + 6 = -10$

A. $m = 4$

B. $m = -4$

C. $m = 1$

D. $m = -1$

SHOW YOUR WORK

6. $32 - y = 21$

A. $y = 11$

B. $y = -11$

C. $y = 9$

D. $y = 13$

SHOW YOUR WORK

7. $\dfrac{n}{4} - 11 = -5$

A. $n = -24$

B. $n = -6$

C. $n = 24$

D. $n = 6$

SHOW YOUR WORK

8. $x + 2 > -8$

A. $x < -10$

B. $x > 10$

C. $x > -6$

D. $x > -10$

SHOW YOUR WORK

9. $2x - 4 < 14$

A. $x < 9$

B. $x > 9$

C. $x < -9$

D. $x > -9$

SHOW YOUR WORK

10. $\dfrac{a}{6} < 3$

    A. $a > -18$

    B. $a < -18$

    C. $a < 18$

    D. $a > 18$

SHOW YOUR WORK

11. $-4b + 5 \geq 21$

    A. $b \geq 4$

    B. $b \leq 4$

    C. $b \geq -4$

    D. $b \leq -4$

SHOW YOUR WORK

12. $c - 15 > -5$

    A. $c < 10$

    B. $c > 10$

    C. $c > 20$

    D. $c < 20$

SHOW YOUR WORK

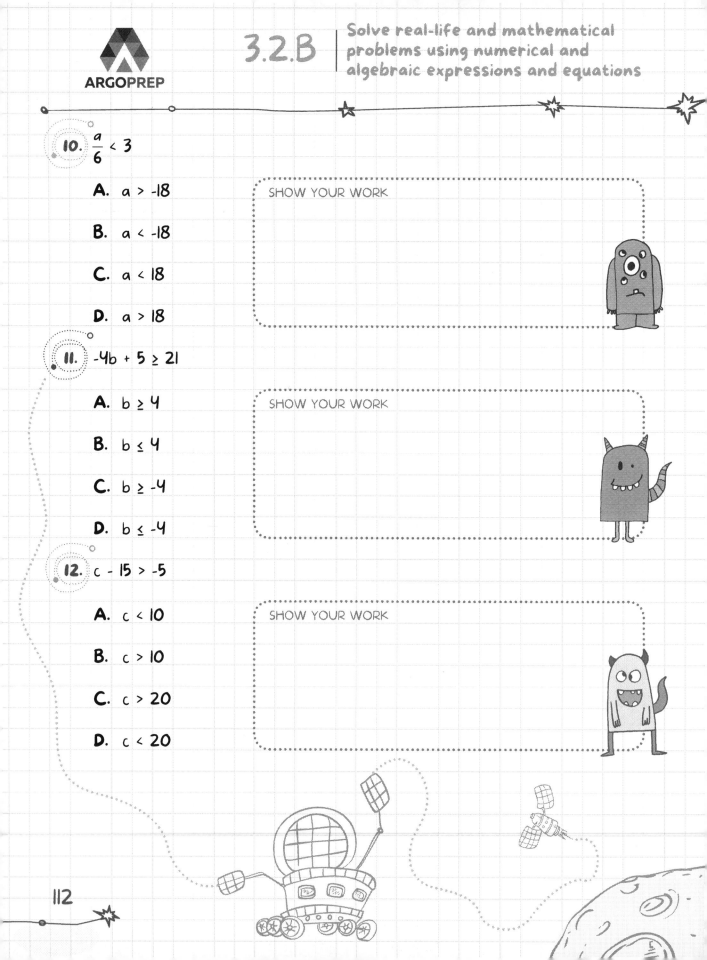

13. $\dfrac{b}{2} - 7 \geq -3$

A. $b \geq 8$

B. $b \leq 8$

C. $b \leq 4$

D. $b \geq 4$

SHOW YOUR WORK

14. $4x - 6 < -10$

A. $x < -1$

B. $x > -1$

C. $x < 1$

D. $x > 1$

SHOW YOUR WORK

15. Erika wants to save $350. She has $85, and plans to save $16 each month. Write an equation to determine x, the number of months it will take Erika to save $350.

SHOW YOUR WORK

16. The perimeter of a rectangle is **61.3** centimeters. One pair of parallel sides have a combined width of **28.84** centimeters.
What is length of this rectangle?

A. 14.42

B. 16.23

C. 30.65

D. 32.46

SHOW YOUR WORK

17. Elijah has a collection of **75** pennies, **30** nickels, and some dimes which total **$5.45**. How many dimes does he have in his collection?

A. 12

B. 3.20

C. 3

D. 32

SHOW YOUR WORK

18. Ryan wants to run more than **25** miles in **8** days. On the first day, he runs **3.4** miles. Write an inequality to represent how many more miles, *x*, Ryan needs to run.

SHOW YOUR WORK

19. Conor is playing a video game where every 1 coin collected gives him **20** points. He has collected **860** points, and needs **1,000** points to reach the next level. How many coins does he need to collect?

A. 5

B. 6

SHOW YOUR WORK

C. 7

D. 8

20. A classroom has **12** desks and some tables. Four students can be seated at each table, and there are **32** students in the class. How many tables does the room need to have for everyone to have a seat?

A. 4

SHOW YOUR WORK

B. 5

C. 6

D. 7

NOTES

ARGOPREP

1. Simplify. 15b - 6b + 12c + 8c

    A. 9b + 20c

    B. 9b - 20c

    C. 11b

    D. 29c

SHOW YOUR WORK

2. Simplify. 42c - 10c - 6d - 10d

    A. 48c - 48d

    B. -16d

    C. 16c

    D. 32c - 16d

SHOW YOUR WORK

3. Factor. 32m + 48n - 72

    A. 8(4m + 6n + 9)

    B. 4(8m + 6n - 9)

    C. 8(4m + 6n - 9)

    D. 4(8m + 6n + 9)

SHOW YOUR WORK

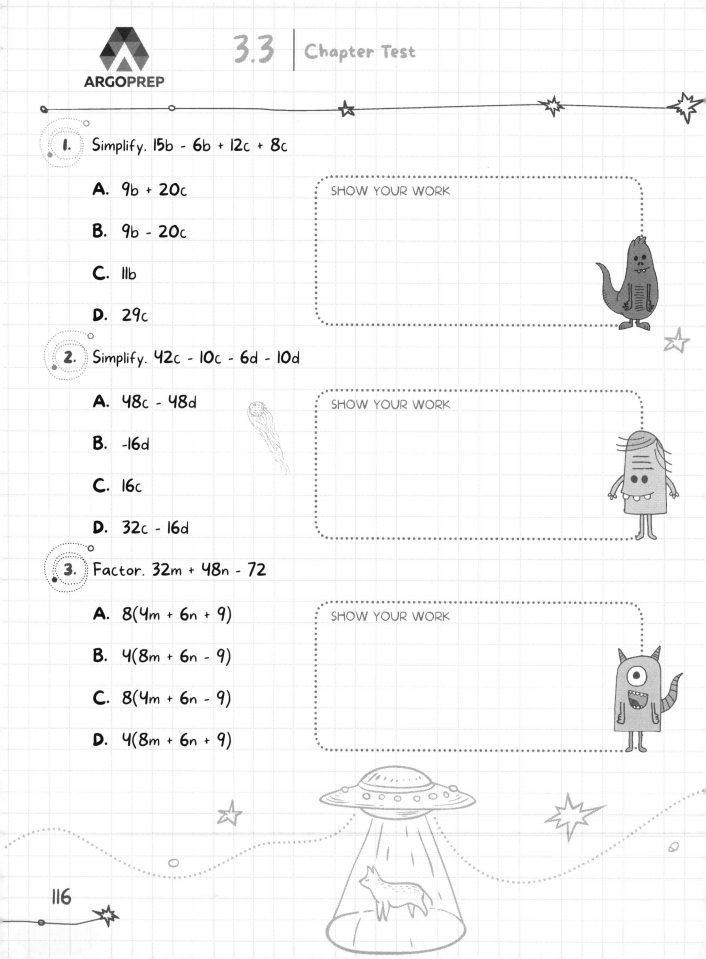

4. Factor. -120b + 50c - 60d

    A. 10(12b - 5c + 6d)

    B. -10(12b - 5c + 6d)

    C. -10(12b + 5c + 6d)

    D. 10(12b - 5c - 6d)

SHOW YOUR WORK

5. Distribute. 6(x - 2y + 5)

    A. 6x - 12y + 30

    B. 6x + 12y - 30

    C. -6x - 12y - 30

    D. 6x + 12y + 30

SHOW YOUR WORK

6. The product of a variable g and 4, divided by 6

    A. 4g + 6

    B. $\dfrac{6g}{4}$

    C. $\dfrac{24}{g}$

    D. $\dfrac{4g}{6}$

SHOW YOUR WORK

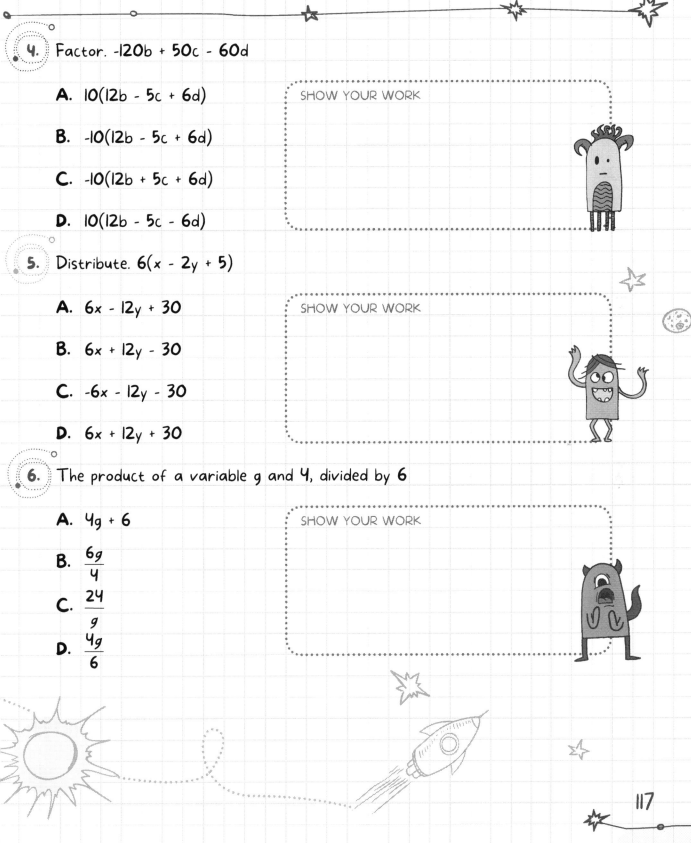

7. Nine less than the product of a number and five

A. $45 + n$

B. $9n - 5$

C. $5n - 9$

D. $45 - n$

SHOW YOUR WORK

8. Thirteen less than a number

A. $13 - n$

B. $n - 13$

C. $13n$

D. $\dfrac{13}{a}$

SHOW YOUR WORK

9. Six more than a number divided by 3

A. $\dfrac{n}{3} + 6$

B. $6n - 3$

C. $3n - 6$

D. $\dfrac{6}{n} - 3$

SHOW YOUR WORK

10. A garden has a width of 4. Write an expression that illustrates its area.

A. L + 4

B. 2L + 8

C. 4L

D. 2L

SHOW YOUR WORK

11. $-\dfrac{4}{5} + 0.65 =$

A. $-\dfrac{23}{20}$

B. $\dfrac{23}{20}$

C. $\dfrac{3}{20}$

D. $-\dfrac{3}{20}$

SHOW YOUR WORK

12. $4.25 \times \dfrac{1}{5} =$

A. 4.85

B. 0.85

C. 4.65

D. 20.25

SHOW YOUR WORK

13. $4^2 - (\frac{1}{2} \times 8 + 3.75) =$

A. $7\frac{1}{2}$

B. $7\frac{3}{4}$

C. $8\frac{1}{4}$

D. $8\frac{1}{2}$

SHOW YOUR WORK

14. Which form is equivalent to **86%**

A. $\frac{43}{50}$

B. $\frac{93}{100}$

C. 8.6

D. 4.3

SHOW YOUR WORK

15. Eric spends **$120** buying clothes. He spent $\frac{3}{4}$ of his money on pants and the rest on shirts and a hat. If the hat was **$11.50** and he bought **2** shirts, how much was each shirt?

A. $9.25

B. $18.50

C. $19.75

D. $10

SHOW YOUR WORK

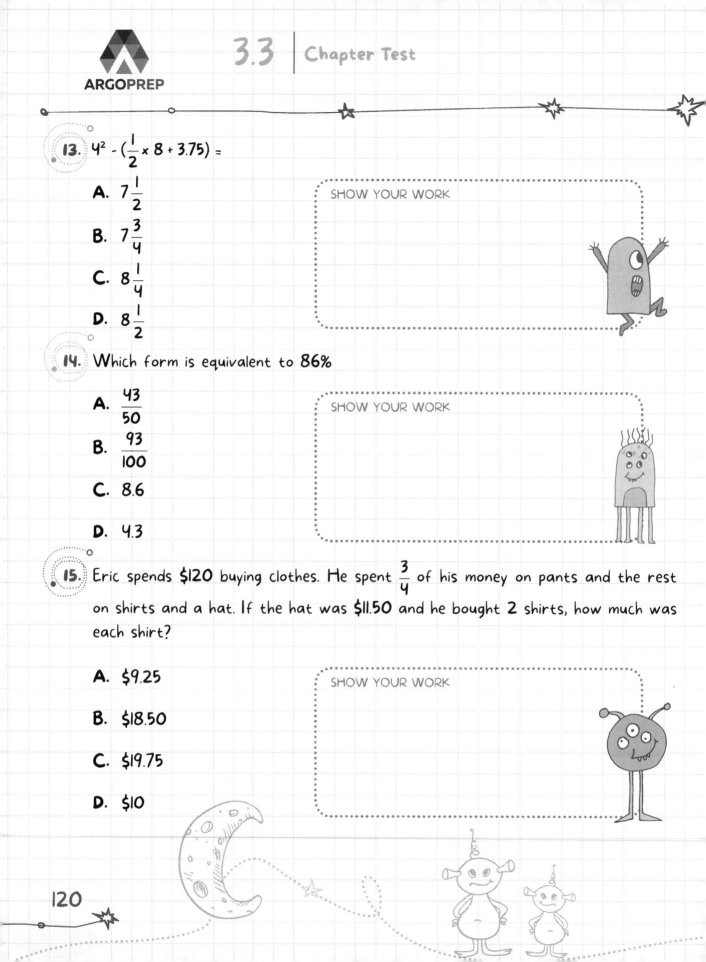

16. The temperature in a city decreases 12 degrees between 4 pm and 7 pm, then rose 16 degrees by 9 am the next morning. If the temperature at 9 am is -6°F, is the temperature the night before more or less than 0°F? Justify your answer.

SHOW YOUR WORK

17. $5n - 6 = -21$

A. $n = -5$

B. $n = 5$

C. $n = -3$

D. $n = 3$

SHOW YOUR WORK

18. $x + 22 = -8$

A. $x = 30$

B. $x = -30$

C. $x = 28$

D. $x = -28$

SHOW YOUR WORK

19. $-4m + 7 > -9$

A. $m < 4$

B. $m > 4$

C. $m < -4$

D. $m > -4$

SHOW YOUR WORK

20. Riley is raising money for a fundraiser. She plans to raise $15 each week. Which inequality can be used to determine the number of weeks, w, Riley must raise money to meet a goal of $300?

A. $15w < 300$

B. $15w > 300$

C. $300w < 15$

D. $300w > 15$

SHOW YOUR WORK

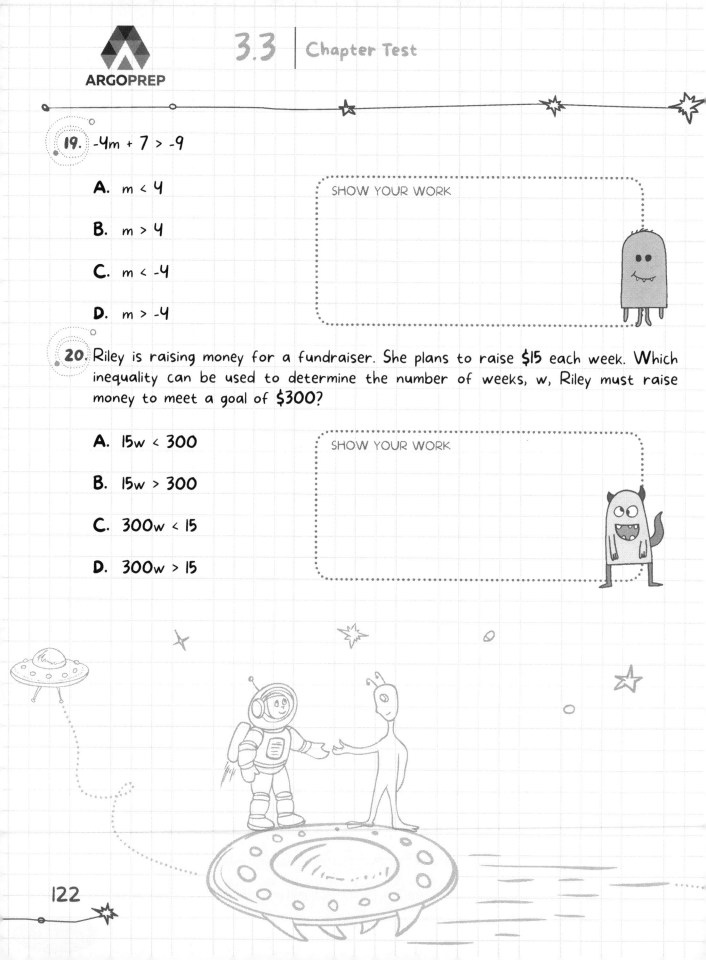

NOTES

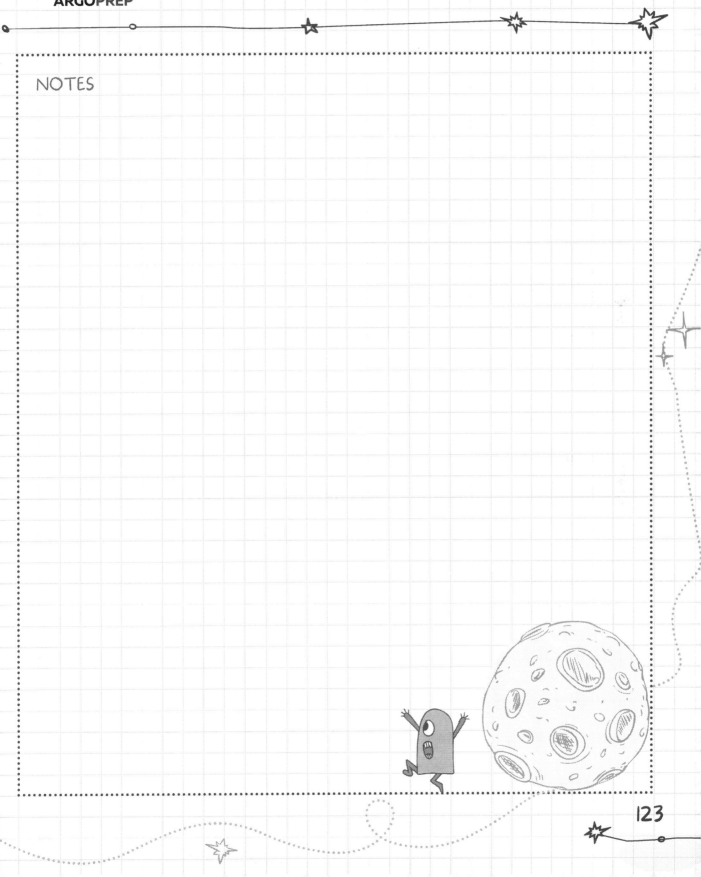

Chapter 4:
Geometry

4.1. Draw construct, and describe geometrical figures and describe the relationships between them. page 126

4.2. Solve real-life and mathematical problems involving angle measure, area, surface area, and volume. page 150

4.3. Chapter Test page 172

Have you ever looked at a map of the U.S.? How do they get the large geographic area of the United States to be represented on such a small area? They use scale drawings.

In the map below, you can see the scale noted in the Gulf of Mexico. When you measure **the distance between two points on the map, about half an inch, it is equal to about 300 miles**.

Let's check out an example. How far is Cuba from South Florida? Measuring, it is about $\frac{3}{4}$ of an inch. $\frac{3}{4}$ of an inch is about **200** miles using the scale.

We can do this with shapes too.

If we have **2** triangles that are proportionate (have the same angle measure), their sides can be related by ratios.

Let's look at an example:

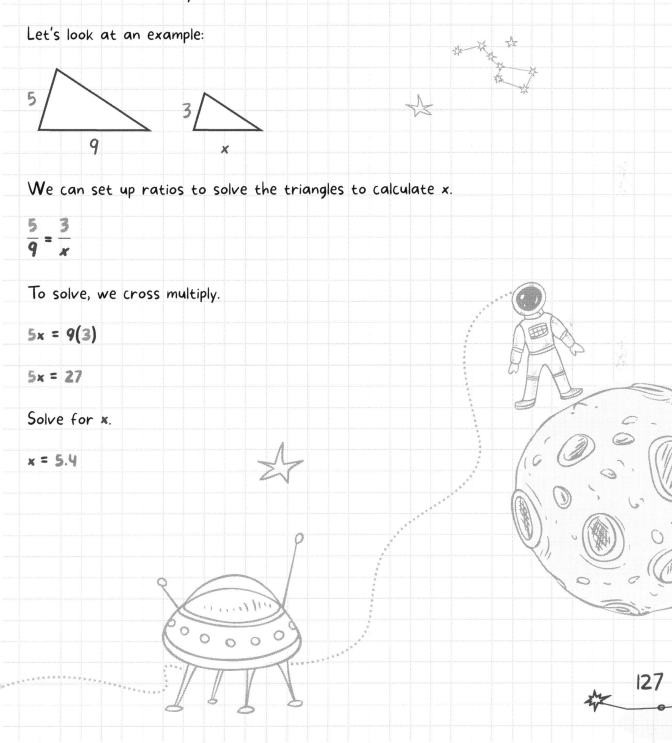

5

9

3

x

We can set up ratios to solve the triangles to calculate x.

$$\frac{5}{9} = \frac{3}{x}$$

To solve, we cross multiply.

$5x = 9(3)$

$5x = 27$

Solve for x.

$x = 5.4$

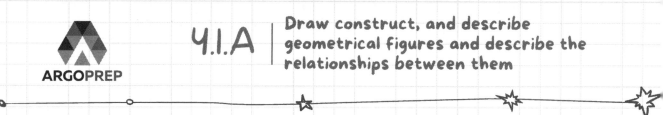
Use the scale on the map to answer the questions 1-5 below, please note, $\frac{1}{2}$ an inch = 300 miles.

1. If the measurement from Little Rock to St. Paul is 0.75 inches on the map, how many miles is it from Little Rock to St. Paul?

A. 450 inches

B. 450 miles

C. 300 miles

D. 300 inches

SHOW YOUR WORK

2. If the measurement from Boise to Harrisburg is **2** inches on the map, how many miles is it from Boise to Harrisburg?

    A. 100 miles

    B. 105 miles

    C. 1200 miles

    D. 1000 miles

SHOW YOUR WORK

3. If the measurement from Bismark to Augusta is 1.5 inches on the map, how many miles is it from Bismark to Augusta?

    A. 900 inches

    B. 9 miles

    C. 90 miles

    D. 900 miles

SHOW YOUR WORK

4. If the measurement from Lincoln to Topeka is 1.75 inches on the map, how many miles is it from Lincoln to Topeka?

    A. 1050 miles

    B. 950 miles

    C. 900 miles

    D. 1000 miles

SHOW YOUR WORK

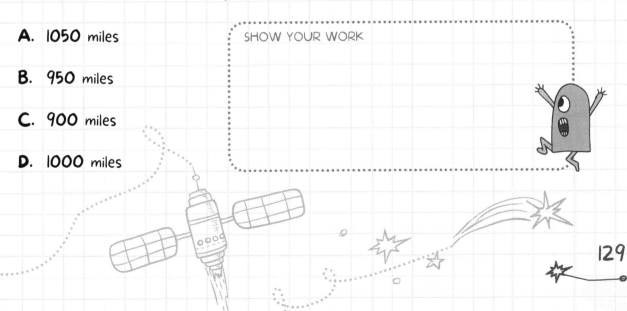

5. If it is about **600** miles from Springfield to Columbus, how many inches are they apart on the map?

A. 1 inch

B. 1.5 inches

C. 2 inches

D. 2.5 inches

SHOW YOUR WORK

6. Elizabeth is creating a scale model of her kitchen. The scale she creates shows 1 inch = **5** feet. If her kitchen is **40** feet long, how many inches should her drawing be?

A. 7 inches

B. 8 inches

C. 6 inches

D. 5 inches

SHOW YOUR WORK

7. Elizabeth is creating a scale model of her kitchen. The scale she creates shows 1 inch= **5** feet. She adds an island to her drawing that is 1.5 inches long. How long is the island in real life?

A. 1 foot

B. 2.5 feet

C. 5 feet

D. 7.5 feet

SHOW YOUR WORK

8. Mitchell drew this model of his bedroom. He wants to buy a bookshelf to put between his dresser and bed. If the bookshelf is 12 feet long, will it fit in between the dresser and bed? Justify your answer.

Dresser — 1.25 in. — Bed

Desk

Door

Scale

$\frac{1}{2}$ inch = 4.75 feet

0 ———— $\frac{1}{2}$ inch

SHOW YOUR WORK

9. Mario draws the attached diagram of his bedroom. If his bed is 9.5 feet long, how long should he make it on his diagram?

Dresser — 1.25 in. — Bed

Desk

Door

Scale

$\frac{1}{2}$ inch = 4.75 feet

0 ———— $\frac{1}{2}$ inch

A. 1 inch

B. 1.5 inches

C. 2 inches

D. 2.5 inches

SHOW YOUR WORK

10. A garden is constructed based on this scale drawing. What is the actual perimeter of the garden? Remember, the perimeter is calculated by adding the length of all the sides.

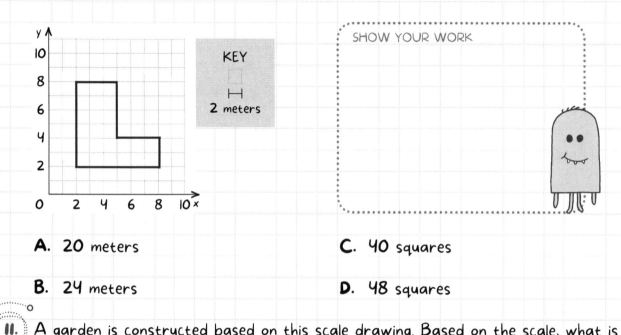

KEY

□

⊢─⊣
2 meters

SHOW YOUR WORK

A. 20 meters

C. 40 squares

B. 24 meters

D. 48 squares

11. A garden is constructed based on this scale drawing. Based on the scale, what is the longest part of the garden?

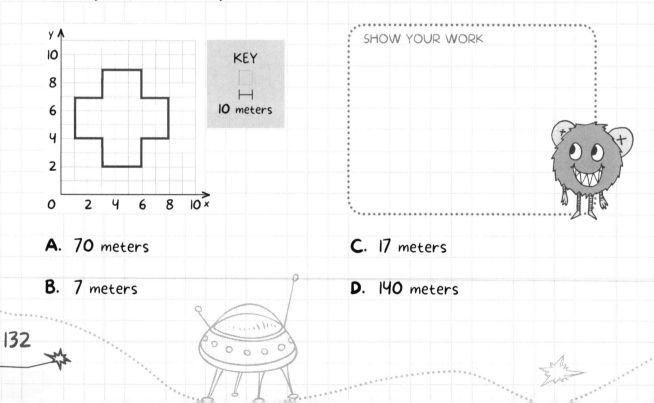

KEY

□

⊢─⊣
10 meters

SHOW YOUR WORK

A. 70 meters

C. 17 meters

B. 7 meters

D. 140 meters

12. Serena is building a model of Mount Everest with the scale of 1 inch = **500** feet. If the mountain is about **29,000** feet tall, how high should she make her model for it to be to scale?

A. 29 feet

B. 3 feet

C. 29 inches

D. 58 inches

SHOW YOUR WORK

13. Based on the scale shown, if segment AD measures **2.5** inches, what is the measurement of segment RV?

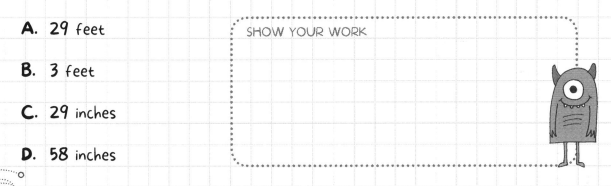

A. 2 inches

B. 3.5 inches

C. 3.75 inches

D. 4 inches

SHOW YOUR WORK

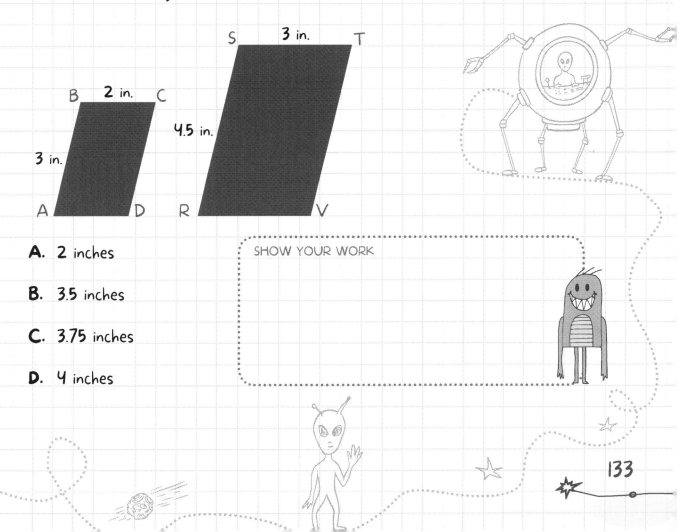

14. Rectangle ABCD is similar to Rectangle RSTV. BC is 12 centimeters. Rectangle RSTV is an enlargement of Rectangle ABCD by a scale factor of 4. What is the measurement of ST?

A. 3 cm

B. 48 cm

C. 6 cm

D. 96 cm

SHOW YOUR WORK

15. What is the measurement of side y?

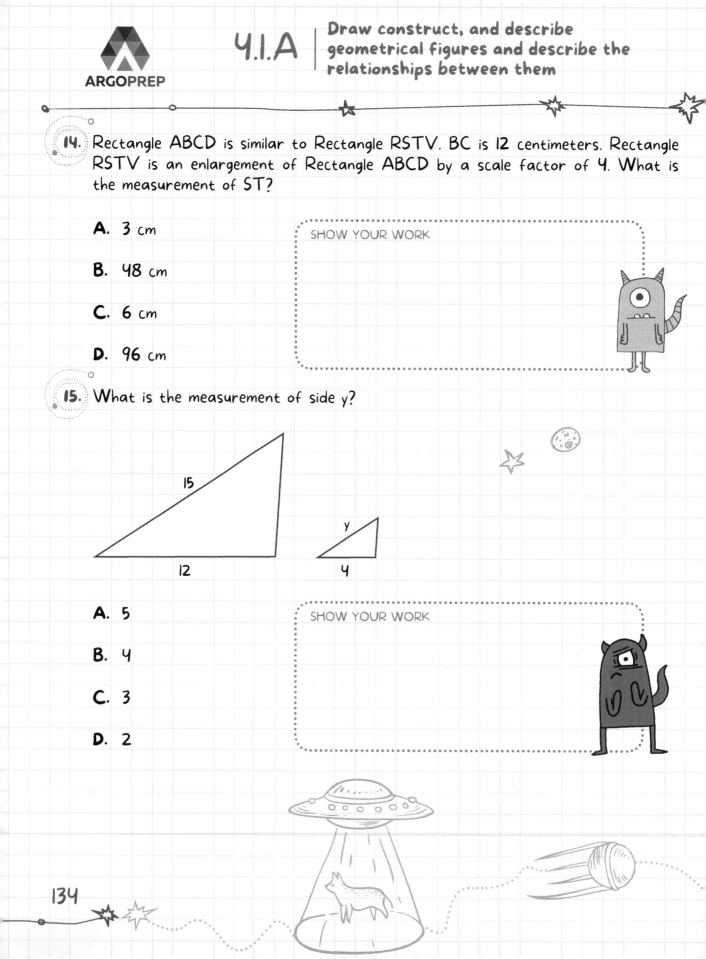

A. 5

B. 4

C. 3

D. 2

SHOW YOUR WORK

Do you remember some of the geometric shapes you learned about in earlier years? Let's review!

Triangle: A shape with three sides and angles that add up to 180°.

Square: A shape with four equal sides and 4 90° angles.

Rectangle: A shape with 2 pairs of equal sides and 4 90° angles.

Parallelogram: A shape with 4 sides and opposite sides parallel.

Pentagon: A shape with 5 sides.

Hexagon: A shape with 6 sides.

Octagon: A shape with 8 sides.

Circle: A shape with no angles or sides; formed by a line that is equidistant from the center of the shape.

Oval: A shape with no angles of sides with a line that is not equisitant from the center of the shape.

Triangles can be further divided based on their angles.

Acute: A triangle formed by three acute angles (angles smaller than 90°).

Right: A triangle formed with 1 angle measuring 90° and 2 angles smaller than 90°.

Obtuse: A triangle formed with 1 obtuse angle (measuring over 90°) and 2 acute angles.

Triangles can also be divided based on their side measurements.

Equilateral: A triangle with three equal sides.

An equilateral triangle will also be an acute triangle with angle measures of **60°**.

Isosceles: A triangle with **2** equal sides.

Isosceles triangles are right or obtuse.

Scalene: A triangle with three unequal sides.

Scalene triangles can be acute, right or obtuse.

If a triangle has **2** sides that are the same length, they have the same angle measurement.

NOTES

1. Which type of triangle has angle measures of **32°, 56°,** and **92°**

A. Acute

B. Right

C. Isosceles

D. Obtuse

SHOW YOUR WORK

2. Which triangle has angle measures of **45°, 45°,** and **90°**

A. Scalene

B. Acute

C. Isosceles

D. Obtuse

SHOW YOUR WORK

3. Which angle measures represents a right triangle?

A. 60°, 60°, 60°

B. 90°, 60°, 30°

C. 45°, 95°, 85°

D. 36°, 44°, 100°

SHOW YOUR WORK

4. Which quadrilateral could have these angle measurements? 104°, 104°, 76°, 76°

A. Parallelogram

B. Square

C. Rectangle

D. Pentagon

SHOW YOUR WORK

5. Which polygon could be created with angle measurements of 78°, 78°, 102°, 102°, 80°, 100°?

A. Rectangle

B. Pentagon

C. Hexagon

D. Octagon

SHOW YOUR WORK

6. Sebastian constructs Triangle ABC. AB is 12 inches, and CA is 12 inches. If the measure of ∠B measures 75°, what does ∠C measure?

A. 75°

B. 150°

C. 30°

D. 105°

SHOW YOUR WORK

7. Jonathan constructs a right triangle and measures angle A using a protractor. What is the measurement of the third angle of the triangle?

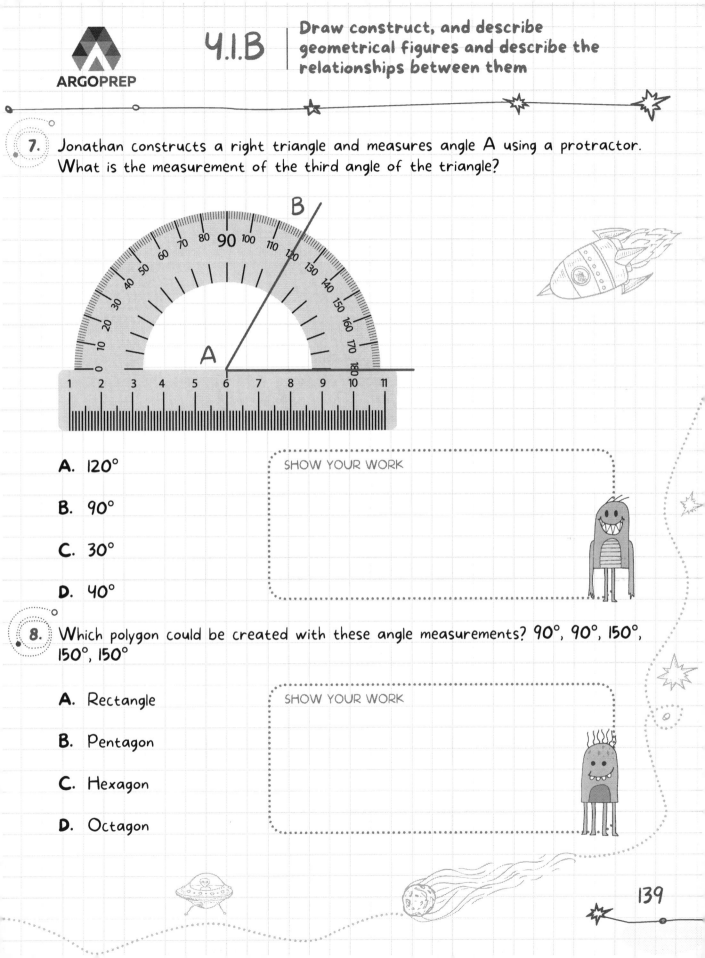

A. 120°

B. 90°

C. 30°

D. 40°

SHOW YOUR WORK

8. Which polygon could be created with these angle measurements? 90°, 90°, 150°, 150°, 150°

A. Rectangle

B. Pentagon

C. Hexagon

D. Octagon

SHOW YOUR WORK

9. Peter is using this protractor to construct △JKL. If angle K measures 110°, what types of triangle did Peter make?

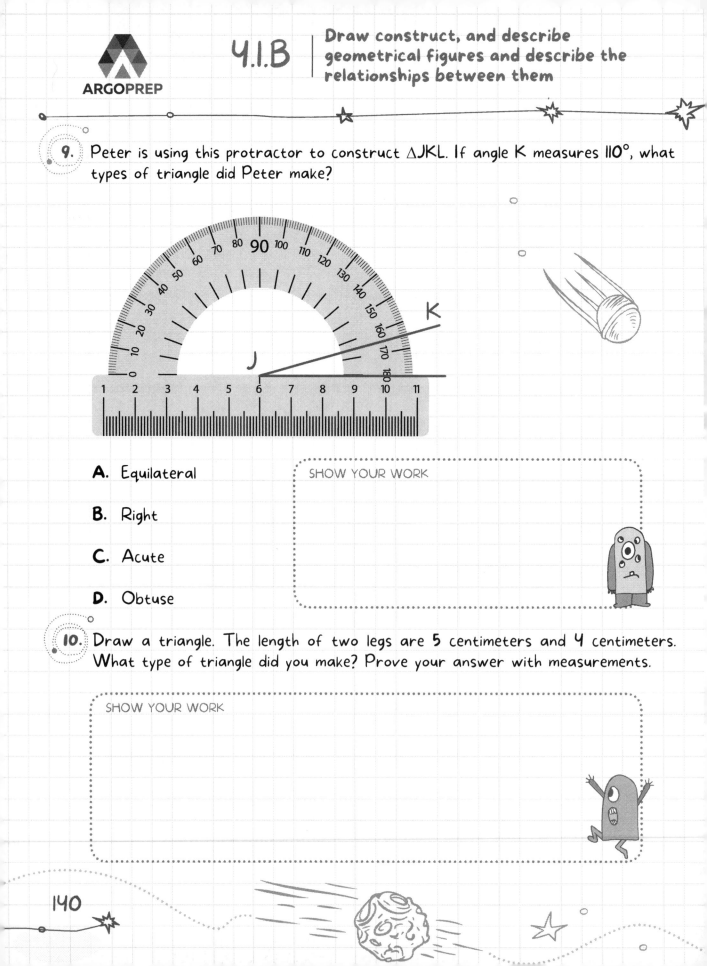

A. Equilateral

B. Right

C. Acute

D. Obtuse

SHOW YOUR WORK

10. Draw a triangle. The length of two legs are **5** centimeters and **4** centimeters. What type of triangle did you make? Prove your answer with measurements.

SHOW YOUR WORK

11. Draw an oval. Explain why it is an oval and not a circle.

SHOW YOUR WORK

12. Draw a parallelogram. Explain why your shape is a parallelogram not a square.

SHOW YOUR WORK

13. Draw a square. Explain why your shape is also a parallelogram.

SHOW YOUR WORK

14. Draw a triangle that is obtuse and scalene.

SHOW YOUR WORK

15. Draw an octagon.

SHOW YOUR WORK

NOTES

Shapes can be **2** dimensional and **3** dimensional. Last lesson, we reviewed **2** dimensional shapes. Let's look at some common **3** dimensional shapes!

Cube - Composed of six equal squares

Rectangular Prism - Composed of six rectangles

Triangular Prism - Two triangle ends connected by three rectangles

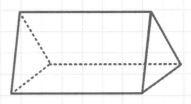

Sphere - A round solid figure

Rectangular Pyramid - A rectangle/square at the base with four triangles that meet at a single point

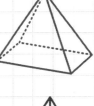

Triangular Pyramid - A triangle at the base with three triangles that meet at a single point

Cylinder - A circle of each of its bases, with straight parallel sides

Cone - A circle at the base and meets at a single point

You can slice any of these figures and view a **2** dimensional shape.

For example, if you cut a cylinder in half, each half has another circle.

NOTES

1. If you slice a cube in half, what shape do you get?

A. Triangle

B. Circle

C. Rectangle

D. Square

SHOW YOUR WORK

2. If you slice a rectangular prism in half horizontally, what shape do you get?

A. Square

B. Triangle

C. Rectangle

D. Circle

SHOW YOUR WORK

3. If you slice a triangular prism in half vertically, what shape do you get?

A. Rectangle

B. Circle

C. Triangle

D. Square

SHOW YOUR WORK

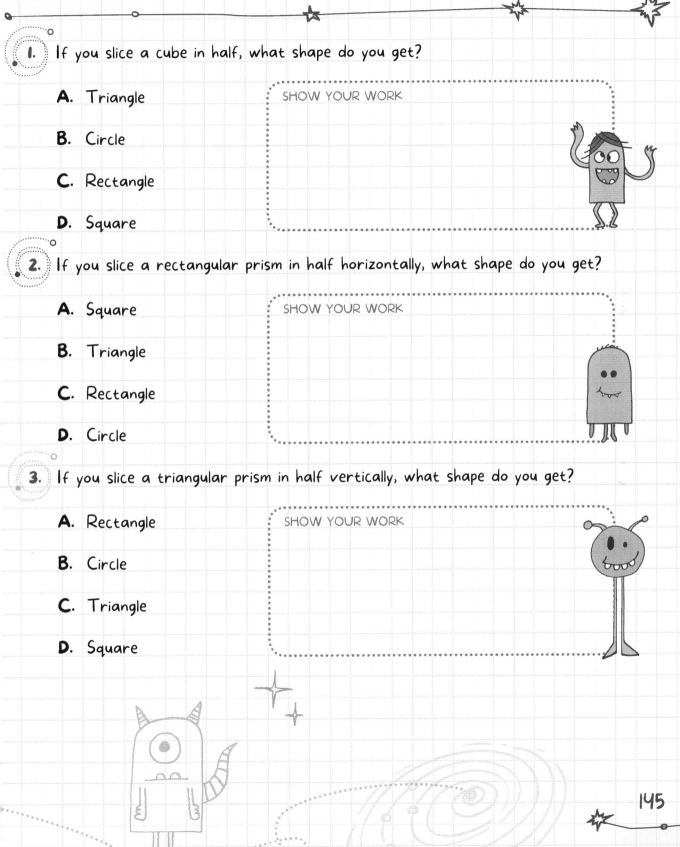

4. If you slice a triangular prism in half horizontally, what shape do you get?

A. Circle

B. Rectangle

C. Square

D. Triangle

SHOW YOUR WORK

5. If you slice a sphere in half, what shape do you get?

A. Rectangle

B. Square

C. Triangle

D. Circle

SHOW YOUR WORK

6. If you slice a rectangular pyramid in half horizonally, what shape do you get?

A. Triangle

B. Circle

C. Trapezoid

D. Rectangle

SHOW YOUR WORK

ARGOPREP

7. If you slice a rectangular pyramid in half vertically, what shape do you get?

A. Triangle

B. Rectangle

C. Square

D. Circle

SHOW YOUR WORK

8. If you slice a triangular pyramid in half horizontally, what shape do you get?

A. Rectangle

B. Triangle

C. Circle

D. Square

SHOW YOUR WORK

9. If you slice a cylinder in half vertically, what shape do you get?

A. Square

B. Triangle

C. Rectangle

D. Circle

SHOW YOUR WORK

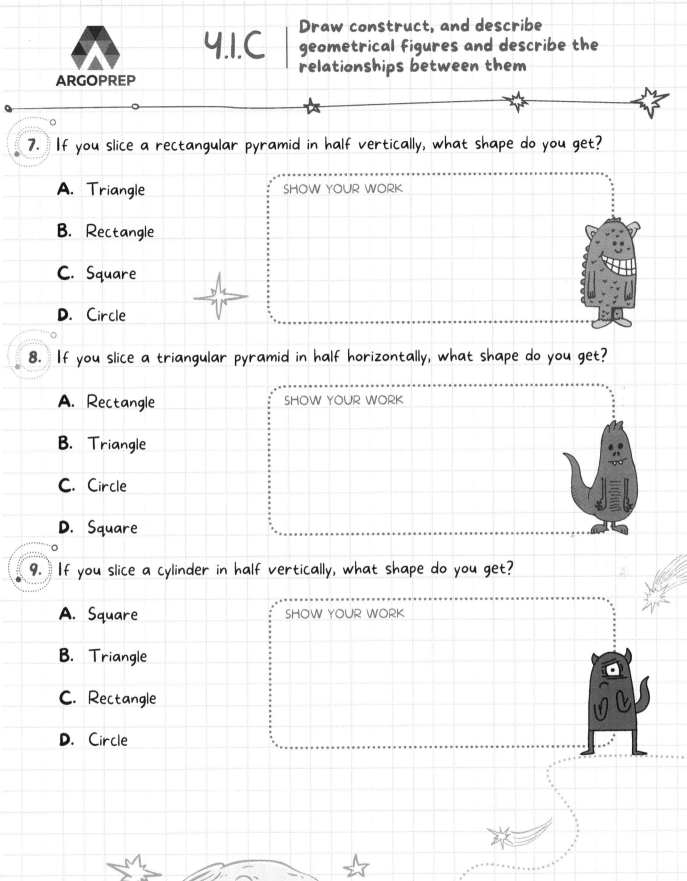

10. If you slice a cylinder in half horizontally, what shape do you get?

A. Triangle

B. Circle

C. Rectangle

D. Square

SHOW YOUR WORK

11. If you slice a cone in half horizontally, what shape do you get?

A. Circle

B. Triangle

C. Square

D. Rectangle

SHOW YOUR WORK

12. If you slice a cone in half vertically, what shape do you get?

A. Square

B. Rectangle

C. Circle

D. Triangle

SHOW YOUR WORK

13. Draw a cylinder.

SHOW YOUR WORK

14. Draw a rectangular pyramid.

SHOW YOUR WORK

15. Draw a triangular prism.

SHOW YOUR WORK

ARGOPREP

4.2.A | Solve real-life and mathematical problems involving angle measure, area, surface area, and volume.

We can use shapes to calculate information about areas of space in real life.

Let's start with a circle.

There are two main measurements that we calculate with circles.

The circumference of a circle is similar to the perimeter of rectangle. It is the **length of the line that surrounds the circle.** To calculate the circumference, you use the formula

Circumference = **2** x π x radius OR π x diameter

Remember the radius of a circle is the length of a line that goes from the center of the circle to a point on the circumference.

The diameter of a circle is a line that goes through the center of a circle and goes from one point on the circle through the center to a point on the other side.

ARGOPREP

4.2.A | Solve real-life and mathematical problems involving angle measure, area, surface area, and volume.

The area of a circle is calculated by the following formula:

Area = π x radius²

Remember, when calculating the circumference or area of a circle, **you can use the value of 3.14 for π.**

Let's look at an example.

Find the area and circumference of a circle with a diameter of 8 cm.

Let's start with circumference.

Circumference = π x diameter

C = **3.14 x 8**

C = **25.12 cm**

Area = π x radius²

To calculate the radius, we half to divide the diameter in half.

A = **3.14 x 4²**

A = **50.24 cm²**

ARGOPREP

4.2.A | Solve real-life and mathematical problems involving angle measure, area, surface area, and volume.

1. What is the circumference of a circle with a diameter of **5** in?

A. 15.7 in

B. 31.4 in

C. 7.85 in

D. 78.5 in

SHOW YOUR WORK

2. What is the circumference of a circle with a radius of **10** in?

A. 62.8 in

B. 31.4 in

C. 15.7 in

D. 47.1 in

SHOW YOUR WORK

3. What is the circumference of a circle with a diameter of **3** m?

A. 28.26 m

B. 4.71m

C. 9.42 m

D. 18.84 m

SHOW YOUR WORK

ARGOPREP

4.2.A | Solve real-life and mathematical problems involving angle measure, area, surface area, and volume.

4. What is the circumference of a circle with a radius of 15 m?

A. 706.5 m

B. 94.2 m

C. 47.1 m

D. 15.7 m

SHOW YOUR WORK

5. What is the area of a circle with a radius of 11 cm?

A. 759.88 cm²

B. 94.99 cm²

C. 189.97 cm²

D. 379.94 cm²

SHOW YOUR WORK

6. What is the area of a circle with a diameter of 6 cm?

A. 9.42 cm²

B. 18.74 cm²

C. 28.26 cm²

D. 113.04 cm²

SHOW YOUR WORK

ARGOPREP

4.2.A | Solve real-life and mathematical problems involving angle measure, area, surface area, and volume.

7. What is the area of a circle with a diameter of 12 m?

A. 18.74 m²

B. 28.26 m²

C. 113.04 m²

D. 452.16 m²

SHOW YOUR WORK

8. What is the area of a circle with a radius of **22** m?

A. 379.94 m²

B. 1519.76 m²

C. 69.08 m²

D. 138.16 m²

SHOW YOUR WORK

9. What is the area of a circle with a diameter of **26** ft?

A. 81.64 ft²

B. 1639.12 ft²

C. 2122.64 ft²

D. 530.66 ft²

SHOW YOUR WORK

ARGOPREP

4.2.A | Solve real-life and mathematical problems involving angle measure, area, surface area, and volume.

10. What is the radius of a circle with an area of **2289.06** cm²?

A. 72.9 cm

B. 729 cm

C. 54 cm

D. 27 cm

SHOW YOUR WORK

11. What is the radius of a circle with a circumference of **18.84** in?

A. 12 in

B. 9 in

C. 6 in

D. 3 in

SHOW YOUR WORK

12. What is the diameter of a circle with an area of **706.5** ft²?

A. 60 ft

B. 45 ft

C. 30 ft

D. 15 ft

SHOW YOUR WORK

ARGOPREP

4.2.A | Solve real-life and mathematical problems involving angle measure, area, surface area, and volume.

13. What is the radius of a circle with a circumference of 31.4 cm?

A. 5 cm

B. 10 cm

C. 15 cm

D. 20 cm

SHOW YOUR WORK

14. What is the diameter of a circle with a circumference of 94.2 m?

A. 15 m

B. 30 m

C. 60 m

D. 90 m

SHOW YOUR WORK

15. What is the radius of a circle with an area of 78.5 in²?

A. 10 in

B. 2.5 in

C. 25 in

D. 5 in

SHOW YOUR WORK

ARGOPREP

4.2.B | Solve real-life and mathematical problems involving angle measure, area, surface area, and volume.

We can classify sets of angles based on their measurements as well as their position relating to other angles.

Supplementary angles are two angles whose sum together adds up to 180°.

Complementary angles are two angles whose sum together adds up to 90°.

Vertical angles are opposite angles made by two intersecting lines and have the same measurement.

Adjacent angles are two angles that have a common vertex and a common side. If you know the total measurement of the angles and one of the adjacent angles, you can calculate the measurement of the other adjacent angle.

We can use what we know about angle placement and measurements to solve equations for unknown angles. Let's look at an example.

Two angles are supplementary. One angle measures 42°. What is the measure of the other angle?

To solve this problem, we need to remember supplementary angles measure 180° together.

So, angle 1 + angle 2 = 180

We know angle 1 = 42

We will define angle 2 as a

So we could rewrite this as the equation a + 42 = 180.

We subtract both sides to get the measurement of angle a, which would be 138°.

4.2.B | Solve real-life and mathematical problems involving angle measure, area, surface area, and volume.

1. Two angles measure 63° and 117°. What type of angles are they?

A. Supplementary

B. Complementary

C. Acute

D. Right

SHOW YOUR WORK

2. Two angles measure 41° and 49°. What type of angles are they?

A. Adjacent

B. Vertical

C. Supplementary

D. Complementary

SHOW YOUR WORK

3. Two types of angles measure 33° and 33°. What type of angles are they?

A. Supplementary

B. Complementary

C. Adjacent

D. Vertical

SHOW YOUR WORK

ARGOPREP

4.2.B | Solve real-life and mathematical problems involving angle measure, area, surface area, and volume.

4. One angle of a set of complementary angles measures **33°**. What is the measure of the other angle?

A. 90°

B. 47°

C. 57°

D. 180°

SHOW YOUR WORK

5. One angle of a set of complementary angles measures **29°**. What is the measure of the other angle?

A. 29°

B. 61°

C. 90°

D. 45°

SHOW YOUR WORK

6. One angle of a set of complementary angles measures **82°**. What is the measure of the other angle?

A. 8°

B. 98°

C. 118°

D. 180°

SHOW YOUR WORK

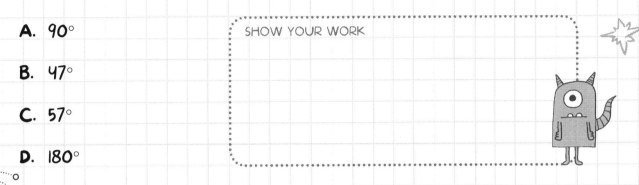

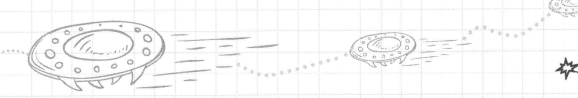

ARGOPREP

4.2.B | Solve real-life and mathematical problems involving angle measure, area, surface area, and volume.

7. One angle of a set of supplementary angles measures 55°. What is the measure of the other angle?

A. 125°

B. 35°

C. 90°

D. 180°

SHOW YOUR WORK

8. One angle of a set of supplementary angles measures 147°. What is the measure of the other angle?

A. 23°

B. 33°

C. 133°

D. 123°

SHOW YOUR WORK

9. One angle of a set of supplementary angles measures 90°. What is the measure of the other angle?

A. 30°

B. 45°

C. 90°

D. 180°

SHOW YOUR WORK

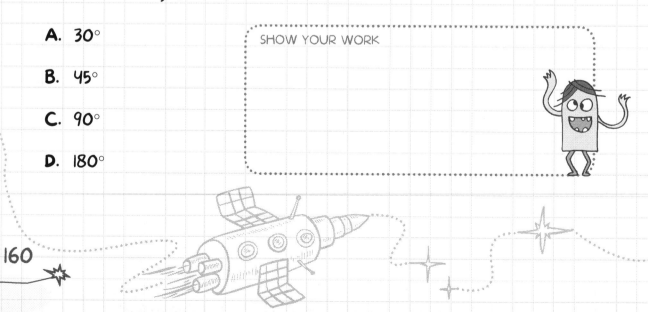

4.2.B | Solve real-life and mathematical problems involving angle measure, area, surface area, and volume.

10. One angle of a set of adjacent angles measures 40°. The adjacent angles measure 80° together. What is the measure of the other angle?

A. 120°

B. 90°

C. 50°

D. 40°

SHOW YOUR WORK

11. One angle of a set of adjacent angles measures 100°. The adjacent angles measure 160° together. What is the measure of the other angle?

A. 90°

B. 100°

C. 60°

D. 120°

SHOW YOUR WORK

12. One angle of a set of adjacent angles measures 23°. The adjacent angles measure 65° together. What is the measure of the other angle?

A. 65°

B. 42°

C. 108°

D. 83°

SHOW YOUR WORK

161

ARGOPREP

4.2.B | Solve real-life and mathematical problems involving angle measure, area, surface area, and volume.

13. Which equation illustrates the unknown angle from a set of supplementary angles with a given angle of **36°**?

    A. $a + 36 = 180$

    B. $180 + 36 = a$

    C. $a + 180 = 36$

    D. $a - 36 = 180$

SHOW YOUR WORK

14. Which equation illustrates the unknown angle from a set of complementary angles with a given angle of **11°**?

    A. $a + 11 = 180$

    B. $a + 11 = 22$

    C. $a + 11 = 90$

    D. $90 + a = 11$

SHOW YOUR WORK

15. Which equation illustrates the unknown angle from a set of adjacent angles with a given angle of **82°** and a total angle measurement of **140°**?

    A. $a + 82 = 180$

    B. $a + 82 = 90$

    C. $a - 82 = 140$

    D. $a + 82 = 140$

SHOW YOUR WORK

ARGOPREP

4.2.C | Solve real-life and mathematical problems involving angle measure, area, surface area, and volume.

We can use what we know about calculating about shapes to solve word problems. First, let's review some terms and formulas.

We can calculate the area of triangles and quadralaterals. Remember, the **area of a shape is the amount of space enclosed by the lines that make up the shape**. When you were younger, you calculated area by counting the squares a shape takes up. Now we can use formulas for area.

Do you remember the formula for the area of a rectangle or square? The formula is **length x width**. But actually, the formula will work for **any quadrilateral** and the **area formula is base x height**.

The formula for the area of a triangle is $\frac{1}{2}$ x base x height.

We can calculate the volume of 3 dimensional figures as well.

Remember, the **volume of a 3 dimensional figure is the amount of space it takes up**. We can use formulas to help us calculate volume.

Volume of a Cylinder = π x r^2 x h

Volume of a Triangular Prism = $\frac{1}{2}$ x b x h x H (where b and h are the base of the prism and H is its height)

Volume of a Rectangular Prism = L x W x H

Volume of a Cone = $\frac{1}{3}$ x π x r^2 x h

ARGOPREP

4.2.C | Solve real-life and mathematical problems involving angle measure, area, surface area, and volume.

We can also use formulas to help us calculate surface area. In 3 dimensional figures, **surface area is is the sum of all the areas of all the shapes that cover the surface of the object**. You can think about it as the wrapping paper that covers the figure. How much wrapping paper would you need to cover the whole shape?

Generally, to calculate surface area, you calculate the area of each face of the figure and add them all together.

You can use the above information to solve word problems based on shapes. Remember to review what kind of shape is being mentioned in the problem as well as what formulas may be helpful to you in solving the problem. You may also want to draw a picture to help you solve the problem!

1. Emily wants to plant two flowers in her garden. One flower in the white triangles and one flower in the blue triangles. How much space will be taken by the flower in the colored triangle?

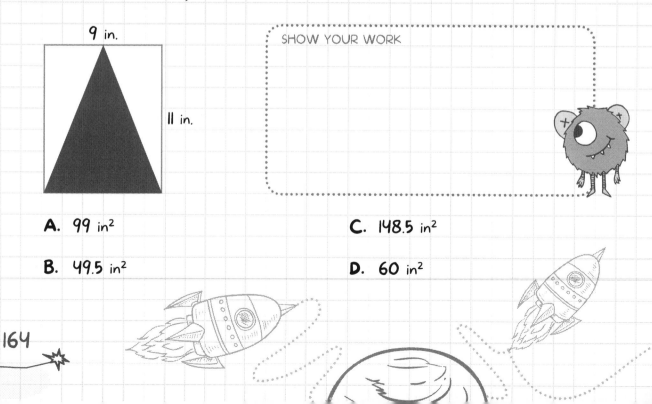

9 in.

11 in.

SHOW YOUR WORK

A. 99 in²

C. 148.5 in²

B. 49.5 in²

D. 60 in²

4.2.C | Solve real-life and mathematical problems involving angle measure, area, surface area, and volume.

ARGOPREP

2. Emily wants to plant two flowers in her garden. One flower in the white triangles and one flower in the blue triangles. How much space will be taken by the flower in the white triangles?

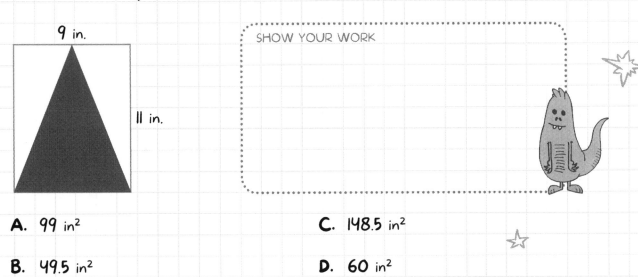

9 in.

11 in.

SHOW YOUR WORK

A. 99 in²

C. 148.5 in²

B. 49.5 in²

D. 60 in²

3. Our town is building a playground. Some of the playground will be covered in grass and some will be covered in sand. If the swing part of the playground is going to be covered in sand, how much be covered in sand?

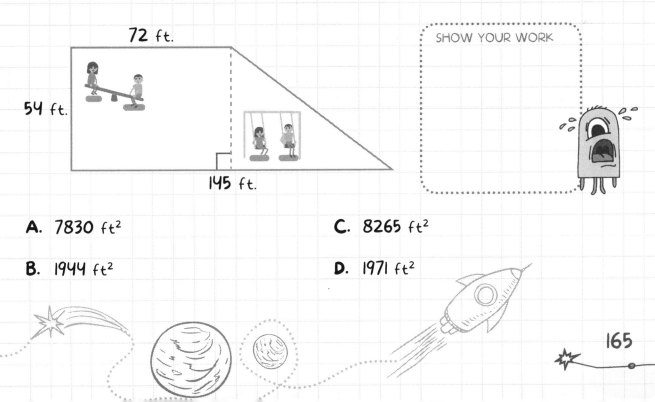

72 ft.

54 ft.

145 ft.

SHOW YOUR WORK

A. 7830 ft²

C. 8265 ft²

B. 1944 ft²

D. 1971 ft²

165

4.2.C | Solve real-life and mathematical problems involving angle measure, area, surface area, and volume.

ARGOPREP

4. Our town is building a playground. Some of the playground will be covered in grass and some will be covered in sand. If the seesaw part of the playground is going to be covered in grass, how much be covered in grass?

72 ft.

54 ft.

145 ft.

SHOW YOUR WORK

A. 1,944 ft²

C. 3,888 ft²

B. 7,830 ft²

D. 10,440 ft²

5. What is the volume of this triangular prism?

12 cm

10 cm

16 cm

14 cm

SHOW YOUR WORK

A. 1,120 cm³

C. 2,240 cm³

B. 960 cm³

D. 130 cm³

ARGOPREP

4.2.C | Solve real-life and mathematical problems involving angle measure, area, surface area, and volume.

6. What is the surface area of this triangular prism?

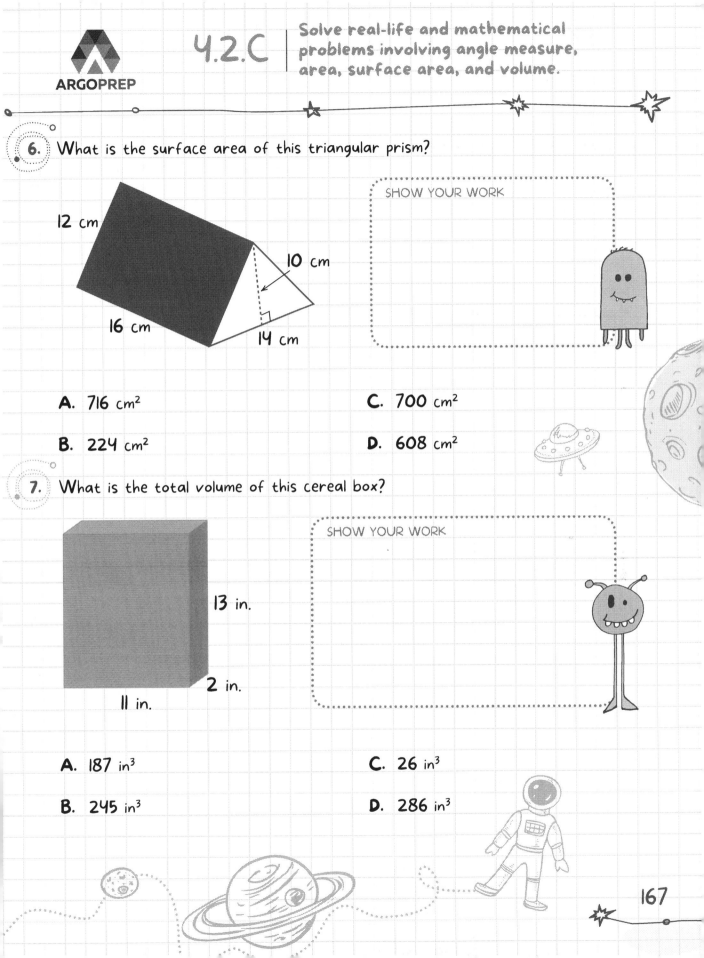

12 cm

10 cm

16 cm

14 cm

SHOW YOUR WORK

A. 716 cm²

C. 700 cm²

B. 224 cm²

D. 608 cm²

7. What is the total volume of this cereal box?

13 in.

2 in.

11 in.

SHOW YOUR WORK

A. 187 in³

C. 26 in³

B. 245 in³

D. 286 in³

8. Elizabeth's mom wants to cover this box with wrapping paper but leave the top open so she can put stuff in and take stuff out. How much wrapping paper does she need?

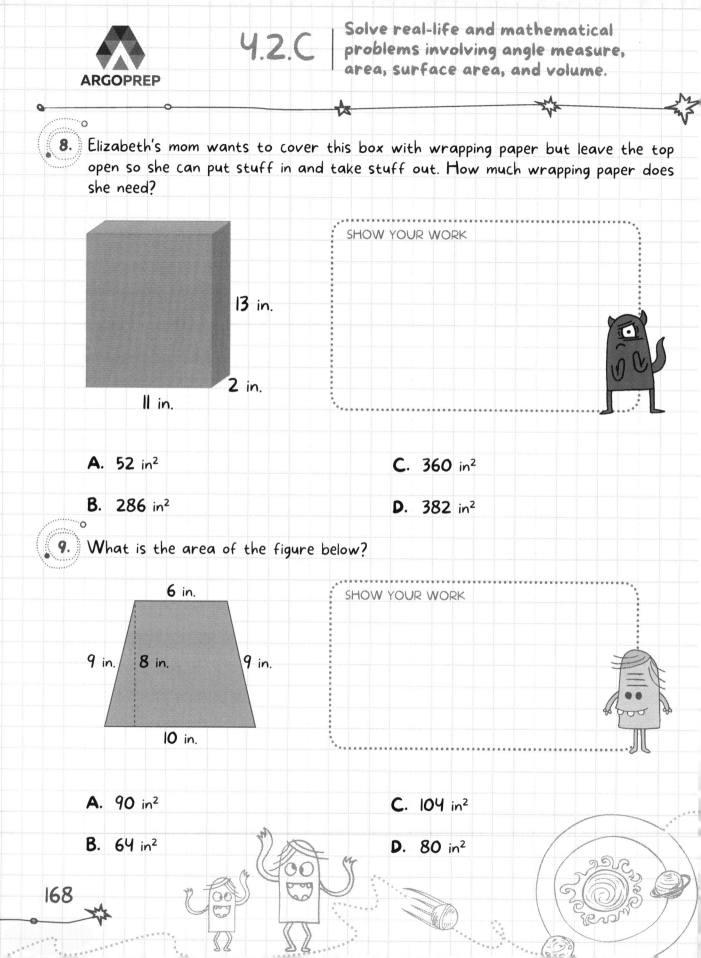

13 in.

2 in.

11 in.

SHOW YOUR WORK

A. 52 in²

B. 286 in²

C. 360 in²

D. 382 in²

9. What is the area of the figure below?

6 in.

9 in. | 8 in. | 9 in.

10 in.

SHOW YOUR WORK

A. 90 in²

B. 64 in²

C. 104 in²

D. 80 in²

4.2.C | Solve real-life and mathematical problems involving angle measure, area, surface area, and volume.

ARGOPREP

10. Albert is wrapping a present for his wife. How much wrapping paper does he need?

6 cm

11 cm

17 cm

A. 34 cm²

B. 355 cm²

C. 1,122 cm²

D. 710 cm²

SHOW YOUR WORK

11. Juan wants to fill this tank with water. How much water will it hold?

6 cm

11 cm

17 cm

A. 1065 cm³

B. 561 cm³

C. 710 cm³

D. 1,122 cm³

SHOW YOUR WORK

169

ARGOPREP

4.2.C | Solve real-life and mathematical problems involving angle measure, area, surface area, and volume.

12. What is the volume of this doll tent?

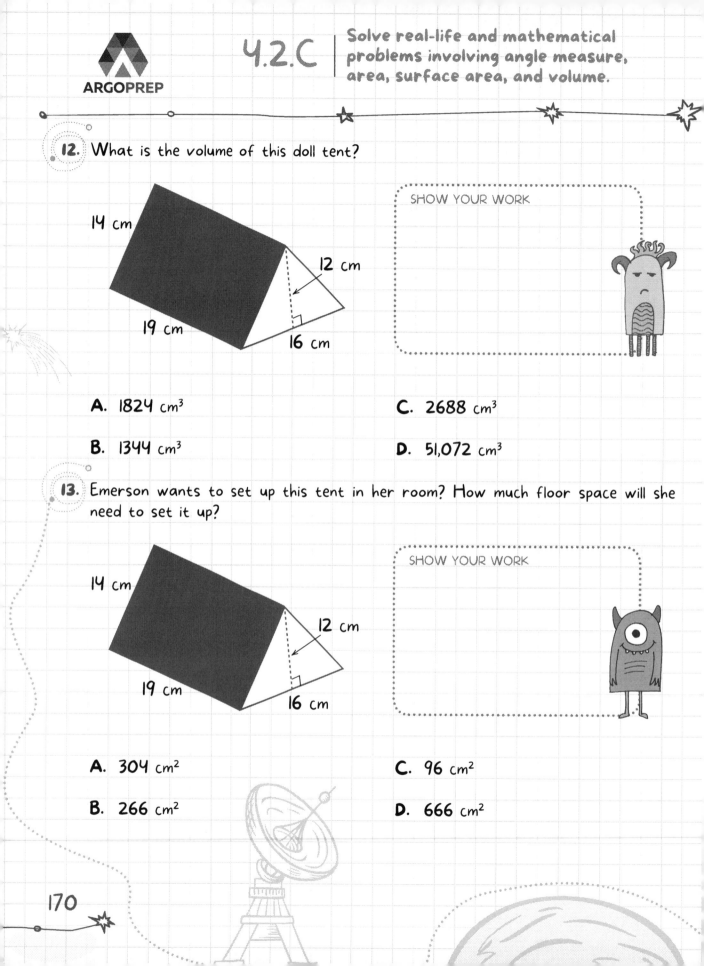

14 cm

12 cm

19 cm

16 cm

SHOW YOUR WORK

A. 1824 cm³

B. 1344 cm³

C. 2688 cm³

D. 51,072 cm³

13. Emerson wants to set up this tent in her room? How much floor space will she need to set it up?

14 cm

12 cm

19 cm

16 cm

SHOW YOUR WORK

A. 304 cm²

B. 266 cm²

C. 96 cm²

D. 666 cm²

ARGOPREP

4.2.C | Solve real-life and mathematical problems involving angle measure, area, surface area, and volume.

14. What is the volume of the rectangular prism part of this figure?

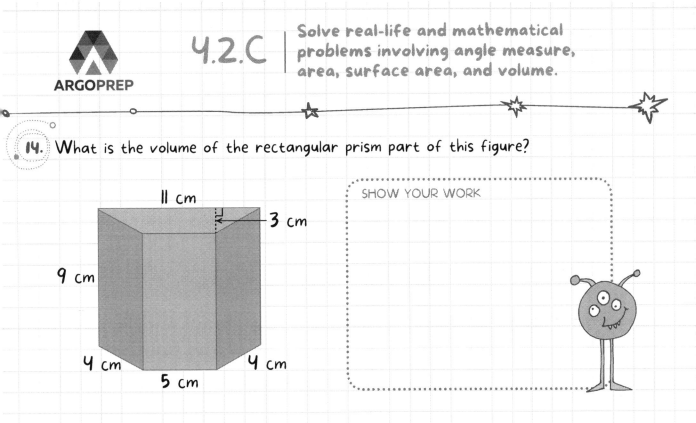

SHOW YOUR WORK

A. 116 cm³

C. 40.5 cm³

B. 81 cm³

D. 135 cm³

15. What is the total volume of this figure? Show your calculations to justify your answer.

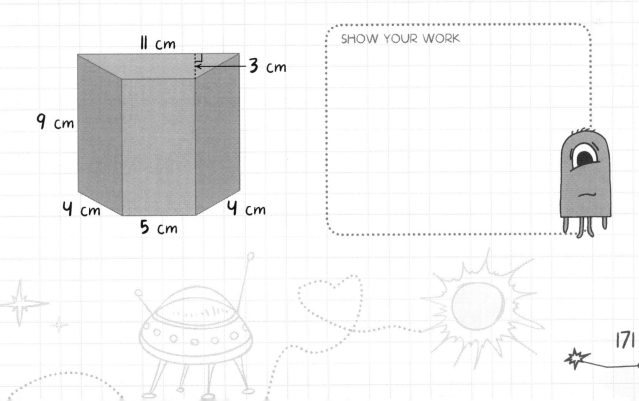

SHOW YOUR WORK

1. Harry draws a map of the Rio Grande. In the scale Harry uses on his map, 0.5 centimeters represents 50 miles. The actual length of the Rio Grande is around 1900 miles. The river Harry starts to draw on his map is 15 centimeters.
How many more centimeters should Harry add to the river on his map so it is an accurate model of the Rio Grande?

A. 12 cm

B. 23 cm

C. 4 cm

D. 8 cm

SHOW YOUR WORK

2. Pentagon ABCDE is a regular polygon with a perimeter of 27.5 inches. Pentagon JKLMN is 3 times larger and similar to Pentagon ABCDE.
How long is each side of Pentagon JKLMN?

A. 16 inches

B. 5 inches

C. 16.5 inches

D. 5.5 inches

SHOW YOUR WORK

3. If side MN measures 5.6 inches, what does side FG measure?

F   G

4.4 in.

J   H

M   5.6 in.   N

3.2 in.

P   O

A. 6.5 inches

B. 7.7 inches

C. 7.5 inches

D. 8 inches

SHOW YOUR WORK

4. Which triangle has angle measures of 120°, 40°, and 20°

A. Obtuse

B. Acute

C. Right

D. Isosceles

SHOW YOUR WORK

5. Which angle measures represents an acute scalene triangle?

A. 53°, 44°, 83°

B. 90°, 26°, 64°

C. 99°, 37°, 44°

D. 88°, 46°, 46°

SHOW YOUR WORK

6. Draw a triangle. The length of one leg is **3** cm, and the length of another leg is **4** cm. Measure the third leg and describe the triangle.

SHOW YOUR WORK

7. If you slice a rectangular prism in half, what shape do you get?

A. Oval

B. Circle

C. Triangle

D. Rectangle

SHOW YOUR WORK

8. If you slice a sphere in half, what shape do you get?

A. Oval

B. Circle

C. Triangle

D. Rectangle

SHOW YOUR WORK

9. If you slice a triangular pyramid in half, what shape do you get?

A. Oval

B. Circle

C. Triangle

D. Rectangle

SHOW YOUR WORK

10. If you slice a rectangular pyramid in half vertically, what shape do you get?

A. Oval

B. Circle

C. Triangle

D. Rectangle

SHOW YOUR WORK

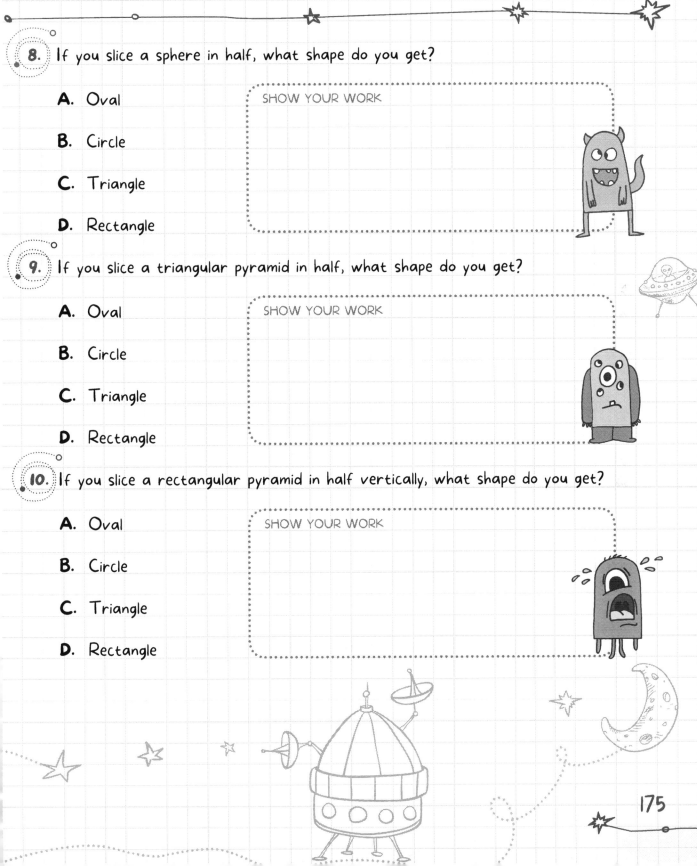

ARGOPREP

11. What is the circumference of a circle with a radius of 14 in?

A. 43.96 in

B. 87.92 in

SHOW YOUR WORK

C. 28 in

D. 615.44 in

12. What is the radius of a circle with a circumference of 106.76 cm?

A. 14 cm

B. 34 cm

SHOW YOUR WORK

C. 10 cm

D. 17 cm

13. What is the area of a circle with a radius of 21 m?

A. 1318.8 m²

B. 131.88 m²

SHOW YOUR WORK

C. 441 m²

D. 1,384.74 m²

14. What is the diameter of a circle with an area of 176.625 in²?

A. 17 in

B. 10 in

C. 15 in

D. 7.5 in

SHOW YOUR WORK

15. What is the measurement of a supplementary angle if it is paired with an angle that is 106°?

A. 35°

B. 74°

C. 84°

D. 64°

SHOW YOUR WORK

16. What is the measurement of an adjacent angle if the other angle measures 119° and the pair of angles measure 200°?

A. 81°

B. 91°

C. 71°

D. 61°

SHOW YOUR WORK

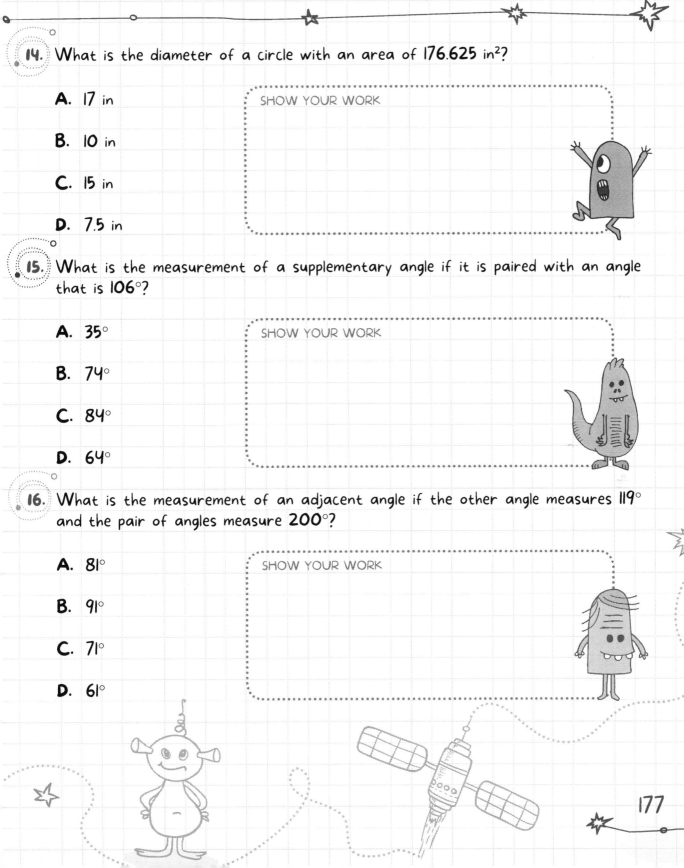

17. What is the equation for an unknown angle if one angle in a pair of complementary angles measures 26°?

A. 90 - 52 = a

B. 90 - 64 = a

C. a + 64 = 26

D. a + 26 = 90

SHOW YOUR WORK

18. Max wants to cover the front of the box with a sign explaining what he is storing inside. To completely cover the front, how large does the sign have to be?

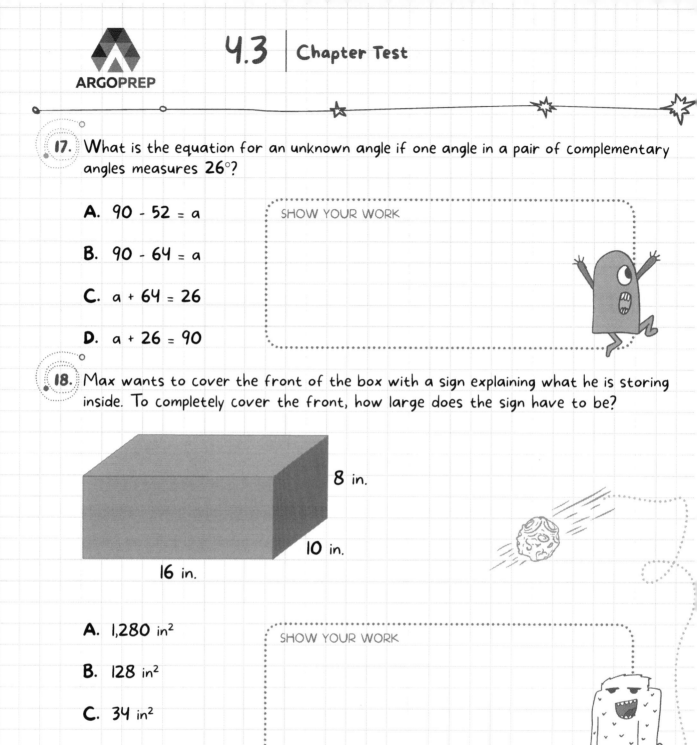

8 in.

10 in.

16 in.

A. 1,280 in²

B. 128 in²

C. 34 in²

D. 340 in²

SHOW YOUR WORK

19. If Maria wants to fill the box $\frac{1}{5}$ of the way with sand, how much volume does she need the sand to cover?

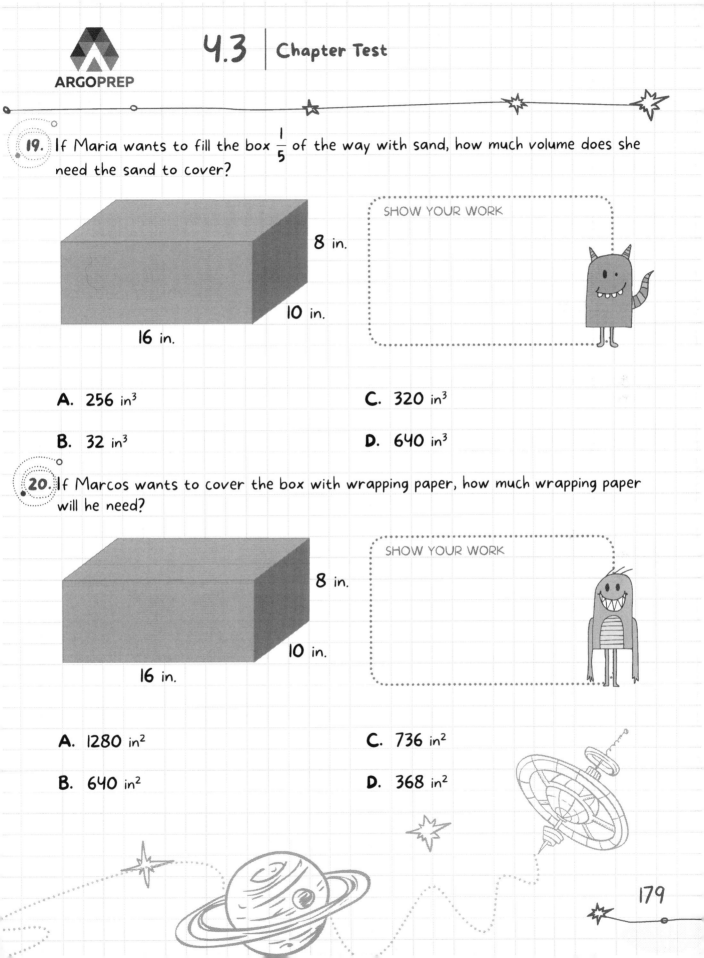

8 in.

10 in.

16 in.

SHOW YOUR WORK

A. 256 in³

C. 320 in³

B. 32 in³

D. 640 in³

20. If Marcos wants to cover the box with wrapping paper, how much wrapping paper will he need?

8 in.

10 in.

16 in.

SHOW YOUR WORK

A. 1280 in²

C. 736 in²

B. 640 in²

D. 368 in²

Chapter 5 :
Statistics & Probability

5.1. Use random sampling to draw inferences about a population. page 182

5.2. Draw informal comparative inferences about two populations. page 201

5.3. Investigate chance processes and develop, use, and evaluate probability models. page 219

5.4. Chapter Test. page 243

ARGOPREP

Let's look at some ways we can use our math skills to study **statistics** and **probability**. Statistics is when we use collect and analyze data in a variety of ways. We do this by looking at a specific group that we collect data about. That group is called the population. We can take a smaller group of the population called a sample. **We can use the sample if it represents that population**. A sample should be a good size to represent the population and randomly selected.

Let's look at an example:

There are 350 sixth grade students, 200 seventh grade students, and 280 eighth grade students at Happy Days Middle School. A survey is being conducted to determine what clubs should be offered to students. Which sample size would be appropriate for surveying all the students at Howell Junior High School?

Taking 1 student from each grade would not be a large enough sample.

Taking a different amount from each grade may be appropriate because there is a different amount of students in each grade.

Which grade has the most students? Sixth grade, so we should take the most sixth grade students.

Which grade has the least students? Seventh grade, so we should take the least amount of seventh grade students.

Which sample would be sufficient?

35 sixth graders, 20 seventh graders, 28 eighth graders

50 sixth graders, 40 seventh graders, 35 eighth graders

The second sample would be better because there are enough students to represent the population.

If we took a sample such as **2 sixth graders**, **10 seventh grades** and **50 eighth graders**, we would consider that sample biased towards the eighth graders.

1. Each day, 1,500 people attend an amusement park. Twice the amount of men attend the park than both women and children. A survey is being conducted to determine which new ride the park should add. Which sample would be biased for surveying all the people at the park?

A. 50 women, 100 men, 25 children

B. 100 women, 200 men, 100 children

C. 30 women, 60 men, 15 children

D. 10 women, 10 men, 20 children

SHOW YOUR WORK

2. There are **600** students in Eric's school. Forty-eight percent of the students are boys, and the rest are girls. Eric collects data on a random sample of students which are representative of the total number of students in his school.
Which response correctly describes Erica's sample?

A. Eric surveys **5** boys and **5** girls from his 1st period class.

B. Eric surveys all **600** boys and girls in his school.

C. Eric surveys the first **50** boys and **50** girls he sees at school.

D. Eric surveys **50** boys in the 7th grade, and **100** girls in the 8th grade.

SHOW YOUR WORK

3. Jason creates this graph to represent the data he collects from a sample population of students in his school.
This data is representative of the **550** students in Jason's school. Which response could represent the number of people in the school who like hot dogs?

Favorite Foods Survey

Nachos 17
Pizza 24
Hamburger 25
Hot Dog 8

SHOW YOUR WORK

A. 10

B. 60

C. 250

D. 542

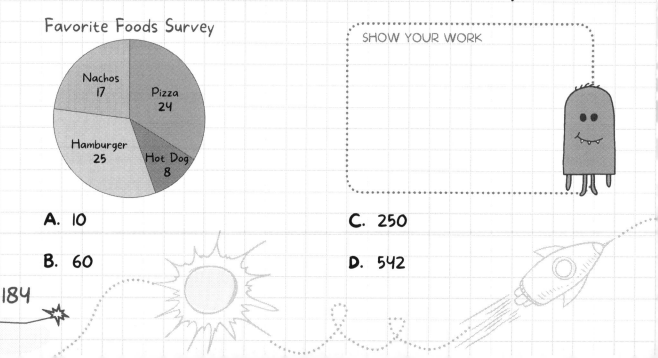

4. Amy creates this graph to represent the data she collects from a sample population of students in her school.
This data is representative of the **360** students in Amy's school. Which response could represent the number of people in the school who like nachos and hamburgers?

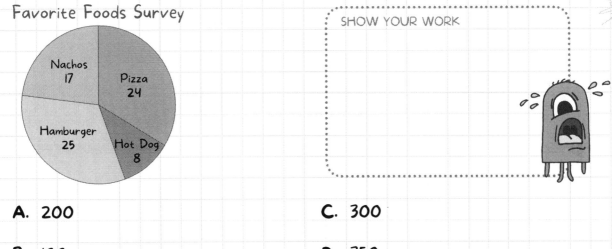

Favorite Foods Survey

Nachos 17
Pizza 24
Hamburger 25
Hot Dog 8

SHOW YOUR WORK

A. 200

C. 300

B. 100

D. 350

5. Jess is collecting data about the number of police officers in each city across America.
Which response describes a representative sample for Jess's data?

A. 40 city police departments from the state she lives in

B. 20 city police departments from each state

C. 1 city police department from each state

D. 30 city police departments from 5 different states

SHOW YOUR WORK

6. Tomas is summarizing data about the city of Washington D.C. Which statement describes the entire population of Washington D.C.?

A. In a study of 45 people, 1 out of every 5 people use public transportation in Washington D.C.

B. A survey is done with 70 people. Thirty percent of the people surveyed live near a beach.

C. Almost 9% of the residents in Washington D.C. are African-American.

D. Seventy-two people respond to a poll. 34% of those who responded are over the age of 35.

SHOW YOUR WORK

7. John is summarizing data about the high school students in his city. There are 4 high schools, with an average of 1,250 students attending each school. Which statement describes the entire population?

A. In a poll of 185 students, over 45% will graduate at the age of 18.

B. Three-fourths of the students are going to college or a university after high school.

C. A survey was conducted with 300 students. Half of the students have experienced online bullying.

D. In a survey with 2,000 students, 3 out of every 5 students would prefer at least one online class.

SHOW YOUR WORK

8. Alice is summarizing data about the number of farms in North America. Which statement describes the entire population?

A. There are 195 farms in North Dakota, Minnesota, and South Dakota.

B. Eighty-percent of the farms in Canada produce dairy milk and cheese.

C. Of the 23 countries and 7 territories making up North America, 910 have farms.

D. A poll of 150 farms shows 7 out of 10 have more than 200 acres.

SHOW YOUR WORK

9. Vanessa is reviewing data about the favorite movies of the 30 students in her class.
Which statement describes a sample population?

A. One-third of the students in Vanessa's class prefer comedies.

B. Fifty percent of the students completed a survey. Of those surveyed, **25%** prefer musicals.

C. Seventeen students prefer action movies, and thirteen students prefer animated movies.

D. Twenty-seven students have been to the movies in the last **30** days.

SHOW YOUR WORK

10. Which statement represents data collected from a sample population?

A. Twenty of the 45 passengers on a train to Dallas are men.

B. In a school survey of 1/3 of the student body, 30% of all students bring lunch from home.

C. Four out of the 5 people in the Gomez family like broccoli.

D. Seventy-five percent of the roads in Chicago have more than 2 lanes.

SHOW YOUR WORK

11. Karl is planning to conduct a survey of the favorite desserts of the students and teachers in his school.
Which response would represent a biased sample population for this survey?

A. Karl plans to survey 15 people in each grade level, and 12 teachers.

B. Karl plans to survey each of the 300 students and 52 teachers in his school.

C. Karl plans to survey 20 students from his math class.

D. Karl plans to survey the first 45 students and 20 teachers he sees.

SHOW YOUR WORK

12. Imani is planning to conduct a survey to determine which pets the people in her town like the most.
Which response describes a representative sample for this survey?

A. Imani plans to survey 40 people at school, the park, the hospital and a grocery store.

B. Imani plans to survey 100 people from her 7th grade class.

C. Imani plans to survey the 8 members of her family.

D. Imani plans to survey 50 people who attend a school play.

SHOW YOUR WORK

13. New York City has a population of 8.5 million people. Mr. Bishop predicts 60% of the population between the ages of 12 and 21 living in New York City have been to a baseball, football or basketball game.
Which response could represent a sample size Mr. Goff used to make this prediction?

A. 20 out of 20 people surveyed

B. 50 out 100 people surveyed

C. 80 out of 400 people surveyed

D. 65 out of 100 people surveyed

SHOW YOUR WORK

14. The results of a poll completed by **100,000** teenagers for their favorite gymnastics team show **6** out of every **7** people believe the **2016** United States Women's gymnastics team was the favorite.

Is this a sample statistic or a general population statistic? Justify your reasoning.

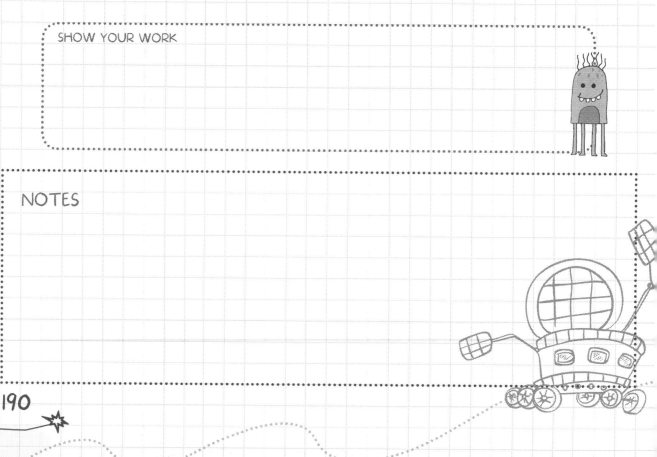

> SHOW YOUR WORK

15. Pedro places **30** marbles inside a bag. The marbles are blue, black, and red. He reaches inside the bag, draws one red and one blue marble, then determines the bag is **50%** red marbles and **50%** blue marbles.

Is Pedro's sample representative of the type of marbles in the bag? Justify your answer.

> SHOW YOUR WORK

NOTES

We can use random samples to make inferences about a population. Statisticians do this by taking a random sample of a population and then reviewing the population to see what in the sample has is common or what is varied. They also take multiple samples of a population to cause their results to be more accurate.

Let's review an example!

Mrs. Soloman's class completes 3 surveys to determine the favorite foods of the students in their school. The results of their surveys are in this table.

Survey	Number of People Surveyed	Favorite Fast Foods		
		Pizza	Burgers	Tacos
A	25	12	9	4
B	20	9	7	4
C	27	13	10	4
Total	72	34	26	12

There are 865 students in Taylor's school.

What conclusions can we draw from this chart?

1 - **Pizza was the most popular choice in each survey**. So, we can say **pizza is the favorite food at Mr. Luzak's school**.

2 - **Tacos were the least popular choice in each survey**. So, we can say that **tacos are not as popular as pizza or burgers**.

1. Devon wants to know how many times the word "the" appears in an article he is reading. He counts the number of times "the" appears in one paragraph.

Devon discovers the word appears 13 times in one paragraph, and the article contains 21 paragraphs.

Approximately how many times does the word "the" appear in the entire article?

A. 280

C. 15

B. 100

D. 62

SHOW YOUR WORK

2. Maria wants to determine the average word length in a book she is reading. She counts the length of each word on one page, and creates this table.

Word Length	Number of Occurrences
2	12
3	18
4	75
5	37
6	45
7	19
8	7
9	3
Total	216

ARGOPREP

Approximately what percent of the book contains words with **5** or more letters?

A. 0.51

B. 51%

C. 35

D. 216

SHOW YOUR WORK

3. Fred collects data about a group of travelers' recent visit to Morocco. He records his data in this table.

Level of Satisfaction with Visit	Number of People
1 - Unsatisfied	2
2 - Somewhat satisfied	5
3 - Satisfied	8
4 - Very satisfied	9

Which generalization could Fredo make based on this data?

A. All people were satisfied with the trip.

B. The majority of people were undecided about the trip.

C. The majority of people were satisfied with the trip.

D. The majority of people were at least satisfied with the trip.

SHOW YOUR WORK

4. Perry buys a bag of blue, red, and green marbles. He draws 10 marbles from a bag. This table shows his results.

Marble Color	Occurrences (Percent)
Blue	60
Red	30
Green	10

Which list shows a reasonable number of blue, red, and green marbles in the entire bag?

A. 45 green, 15 red, 5 blue

B. 45 green, 15 blue, 5 red

C. 45 blue, 15 red, 5 green

D. 45 red, 15 green, 5 blue

SHOW YOUR WORK

5. There are 4 prime numbers between 1 and 10. Based on this data, Taylor predicts there will be _____ prime numbers between 1 and **200**.

A. 100

B. 4

C. 80

D. 20

SHOW YOUR WORK

6. Reilly sells **28** boxes of popcorn and **45** sodas at a football game on Monday night. On Thursday night, she sells **35** boxes of popcorn and **56** sodas.
Which statement could be an accurate prediction about what Reilly will sell at the next football game?

A. She will sell at least **40** boxes of popcorn.

B. She will sell no more than **10** boxes of popcorn.

C. She will sell more popcorn than soda.

D. She will sell at least **100** sodas.

SHOW YOUR WORK

7. On Tuesday, Felicia sells **12** candy bars and **8** sodas to her friends. On Wednesday, Felicia sells **7** candy bars and **5** sodas to her friends.
Which statement could be an accurate prediction about what Felicia will sell to her friends on Thursday?

A. She will sell at least **40** candy bars.

B. She will sell less candy and soda than on Tuesday.

C. She will sell at least **15** sodas.

D. She will sell at least **50** candy bars and sodas.

SHOW YOUR WORK

8. Michael sold **54** children's tickets and **95** adult tickets to a school play two weeks ago. Last week, he sold **30** children's tickets and **53** adult tickets.

Which statement could be an accurate prediction about what the number of children and adult tickets Michael will sell this week?

A. Michael will sell more tickets than he sold last week.

B. Michael will not sell more than **15** tickets.

C. Michael will sell at least **200** tickets.

D. Michael will sell more adult tickets than children tickets.

SHOW YOUR WORK

9. The data in this bar graph shows the different sports played by the students in Ms. Davis's class.

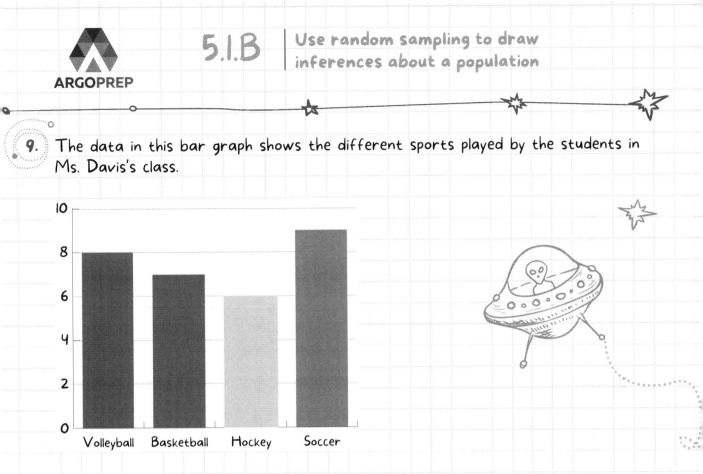

There are **345** students in Ms. Davis's school. Using this data to make inferences about the entire school, how many students play both soccer and volleyball?

A. 30

B. 75

C. 200

D. 50

SHOW YOUR WORK

10. Three out of **5** goats on Mr. McDonald's farm are female. Four out of **7** goats on Mrs. Dell's farm are female.

Using this data, if a farm has **42** goats, approximately how many will be female?

A. 15

B. 20

C. 25

D. 30

SHOW YOUR WORK

11. This table shows the number of male and female flamingos at **5** different zoos.

Male Flamingos	Female Flamingos
10	16
12	18
5	9
7	11
9	14

Using this data, in a larger zoo population of **120** flamingos approximately how many are female?

A. 20

B. 110

C. 10

D. 75

SHOW YOUR WORK

12. This table shows the number of male and female parrots at **5** different zoos.

Male Parrots	Female Parrots
2	5
1	3
1	4
3	7
1	3

Using this data, in a larger zoo population of **20** parrots approximately how many are male?

A. 1

B. 6

C. 12

D. 18

SHOW YOUR WORK

13. Leann reads an article which says 4 out of 5 people prefer using their cell phone to search the Internet.

If there are 3,000 people in Leann's city, approximately how many people prefer using their cell phone to search the Internet?

A. 2,400

B. 1,000

C. 1,800

D. 2,800

SHOW YOUR WORK

14. Harrison polls the families in his neighborhood to determine how many children they have. Thirty-five percent of the families have more than 2 children.

If Harrison polled 200 families, approximately how many families will have more than 2 children?

A. 180

B. 150

C. 30

D. 75

SHOW YOUR WORK

15. Dawn recognizes there are 4 prime numbers between 1 and 10. She estimates there will be 40 prime numbers between 1 and 100.

Do you agree with Dawn? Explain your thinking.

SHOW YOUR WORK

Let's review some common statistics terms!

Distribution - The way the data is spread out.

Statistical Center - The middle point of how the data is distributed.

Statistical Spread - Explains how the data is distributed.

Mean Absolute Deviation - The average difference between each data point and the mean.

Let's apply these to a data set!

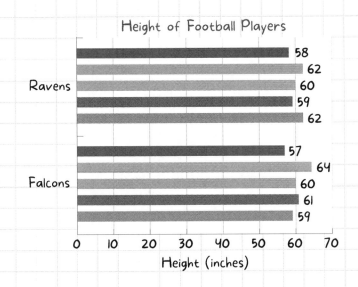

What is the statistical center of the Raven's players? 60 inches

What is the statistical spread of the Falcolns? 64 - 57 = 7 inches

How would you generally describe the spread of the Ravens? Most of the data is located around 60 inches.

What is the lowest height for the Falcons? 57 inches

1. What is the statistical center for Mr Bell's class?

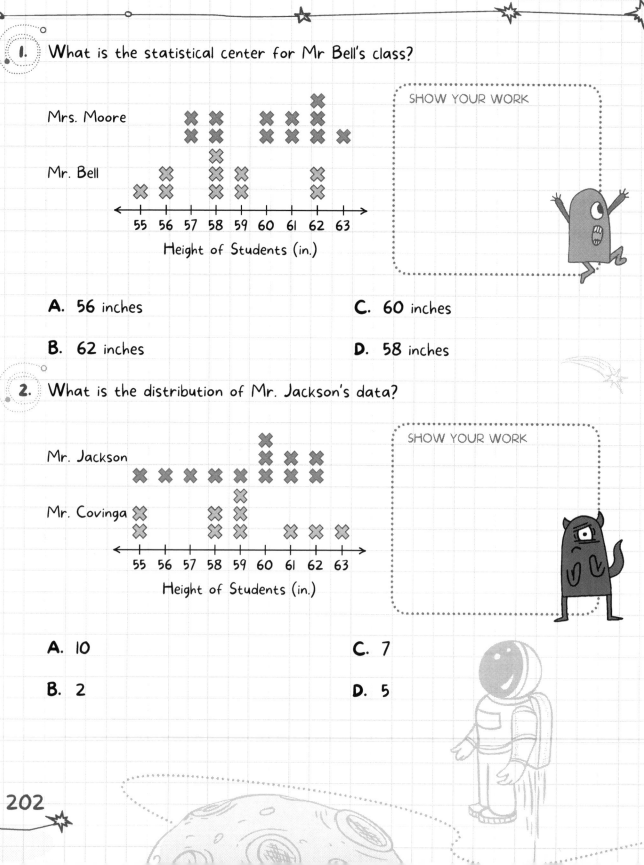

SHOW YOUR WORK

A. 56 inches

C. 60 inches

B. 62 inches

D. 58 inches

2. What is the distribution of Mr. Jackson's data?

SHOW YOUR WORK

A. 10

C. 7

B. 2

D. 5

3. What is the distribution of the data?

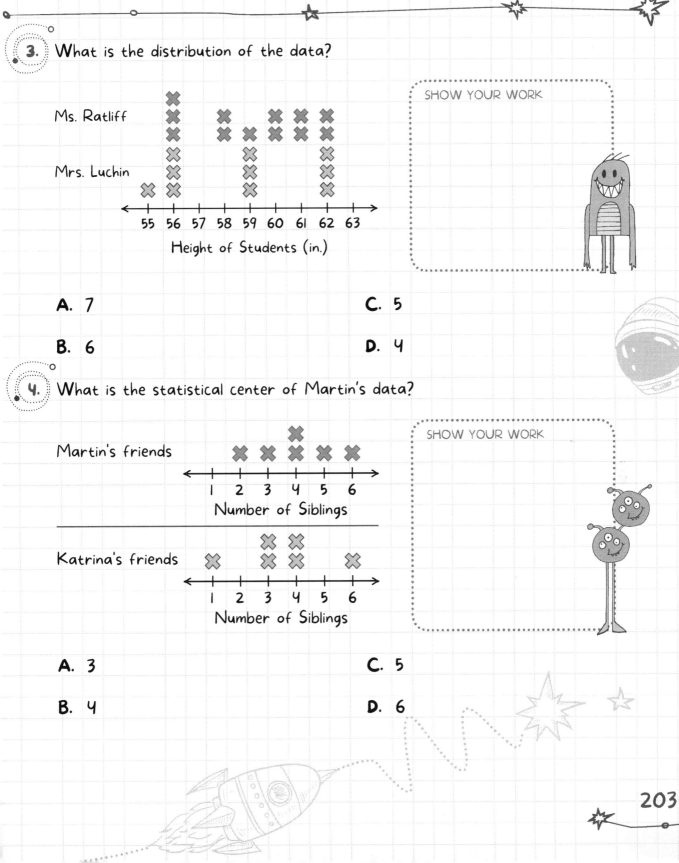

Ms. Ratliff

Mrs. Luchin

55 56 57 58 59 60 61 62 63
Height of Students (in.)

SHOW YOUR WORK

A. 7

C. 5

B. 6

D. 4

4. What is the statistical center of Martin's data?

Martin's friends

1 2 3 4 5 6
Number of Siblings

Katrina's friends

1 2 3 4 5 6
Number of Siblings

SHOW YOUR WORK

A. 3

C. 5

B. 4

D. 6

5. What is Isabel's statistical center?

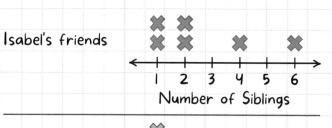

Isabel's friends

Number of Siblings

Pedro's friends

Number of Siblings

A. 2

C. 4

B. 3

D. 5

6. What is Joshua's statistical spread?

Joshua's friends

Number of Siblings

Dante's friends

Number of Siblings

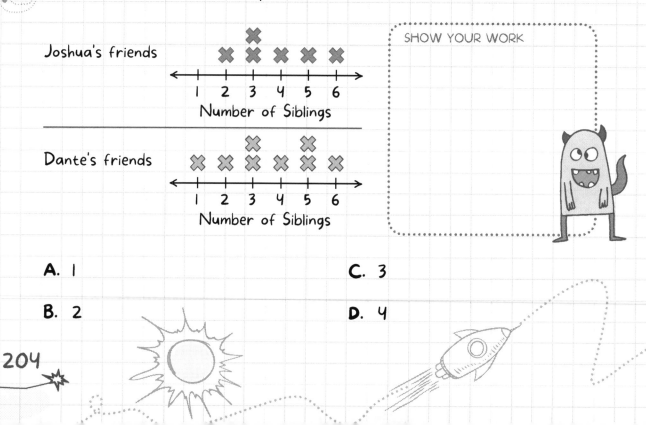

A. 1

C. 3

B. 2

D. 4

7. What is the statistical spread of the sixth grade students data?

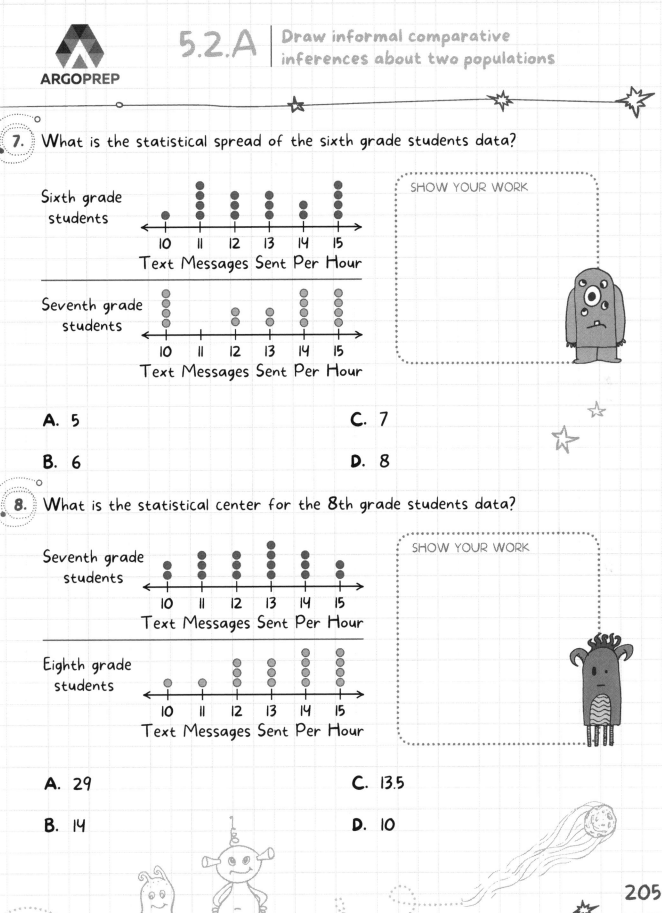

SHOW YOUR WORK

Sixth grade students

Text Messages Sent Per Hour

Seventh grade students

Text Messages Sent Per Hour

A. 5

C. 7

B. 6

D. 8

8. What is the statistical center for the 8th grade students data?

SHOW YOUR WORK

Seventh grade students

Text Messages Sent Per Hour

Eighth grade students

Text Messages Sent Per Hour

A. 29

C. 13.5

B. 14

D. 10

205

9. What is the statistical spread for the Johnsonville Zoo?

Johnsonville
City Zoo

400 425 450 475 500 525
Alligator Weight (pounds)

Calvington
Zoo

400 425 450 475 500 525
Alligator Weight (pounds)

SHOW YOUR WORK

A. 100

C. 150

B. 125

D. 200

10. What is the statistical center for the Overton Zoo?

Thompson
Zoo

400 425 450 475 500 525
Alligator Weight (pounds)

Overton
Zoo

400 425 450 475 500 525
Alligator Weight (pounds)

SHOW YOUR WORK

A. 125

C. 450

B. 400

D. 475

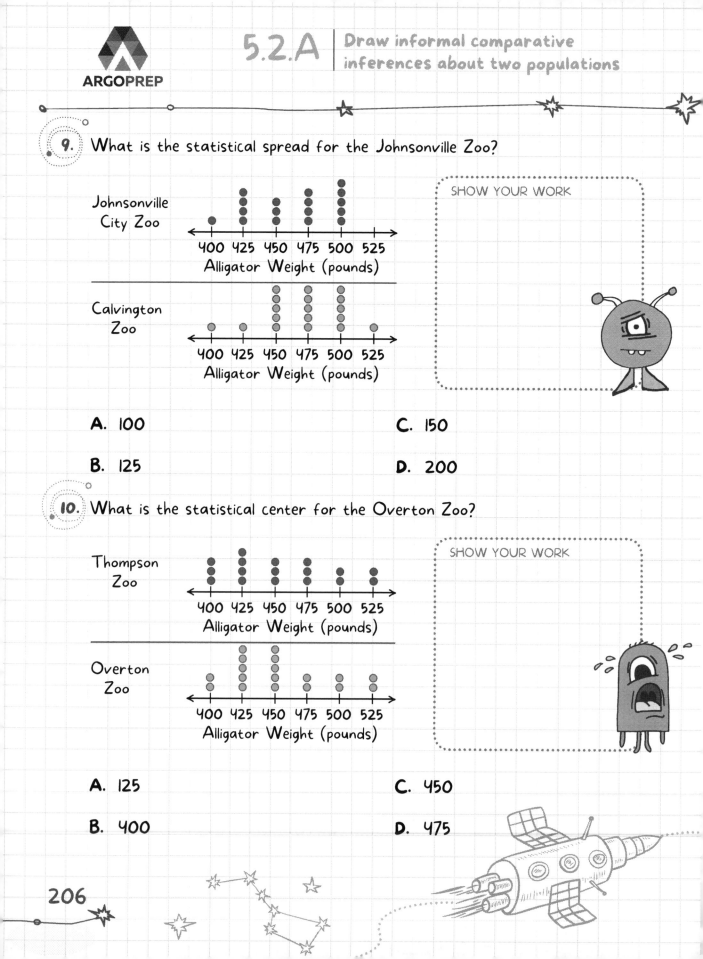

11. What is the statistical center for the Washington Zoo?

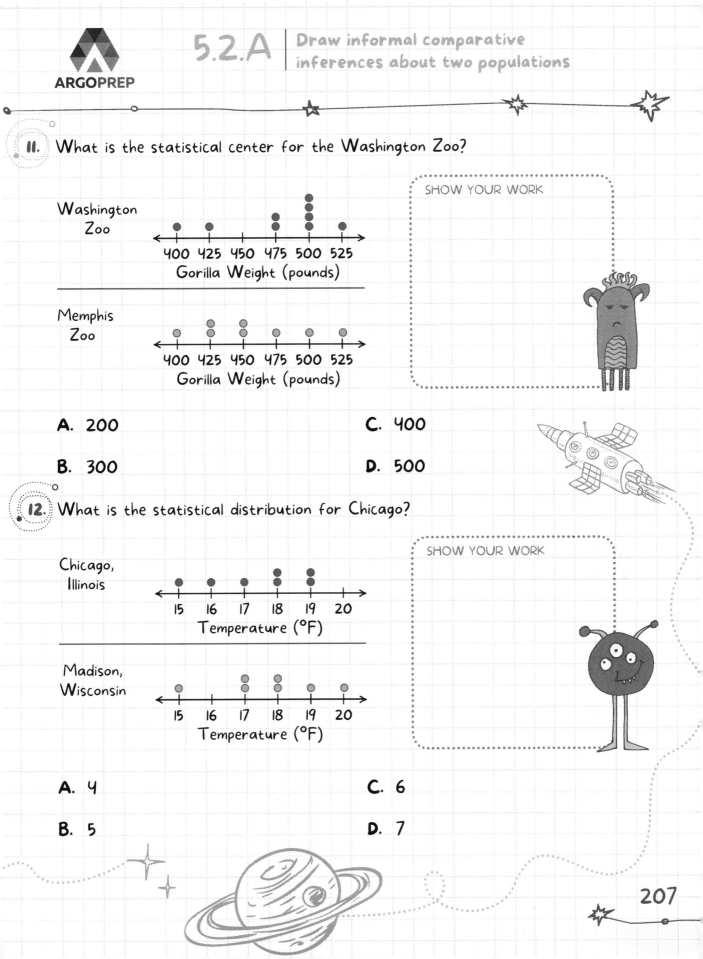

SHOW YOUR WORK

Washington Zoo

Gorilla Weight (pounds)
400 425 450 475 500 525

Memphis Zoo

Gorilla Weight (pounds)
400 425 450 475 500 525

A. 200   **C.** 400

B. 300   **D.** 500

12. What is the statistical distribution for Chicago?

SHOW YOUR WORK

Chicago, Illinois

Temperature (°F)
15 16 17 18 19 20

Madison, Wisconsin

Temperature (°F)
15 16 17 18 19 20

A. 4   **C.** 6

B. 5   **D.** 7

13. What is the statistical spread of Gary?

Gary,
Indiana

```
   15  16  17  18  19  20
        Temperature (°F)
```

Chicago,
Illinois

```
   15  16  17  18  19  20
        Temperature (°F)
```

SHOW YOUR WORK

A. 3

C. 5

B. 4

D. 6

14. What is the statistical center for Canton?

Canton,
Ohio

```
   15  16  17  18  19  20
        Temperature (°F)
```

Milwaukee,
Wisconsin

```
   15  16  17  18  19  20
        Temperature (°F)
```

SHOW YOUR WORK

A. 14

C. 16

B. 15

D. 17

15. What is the statistical center of Ms Wilson's class?

Ms. Wilson's Class

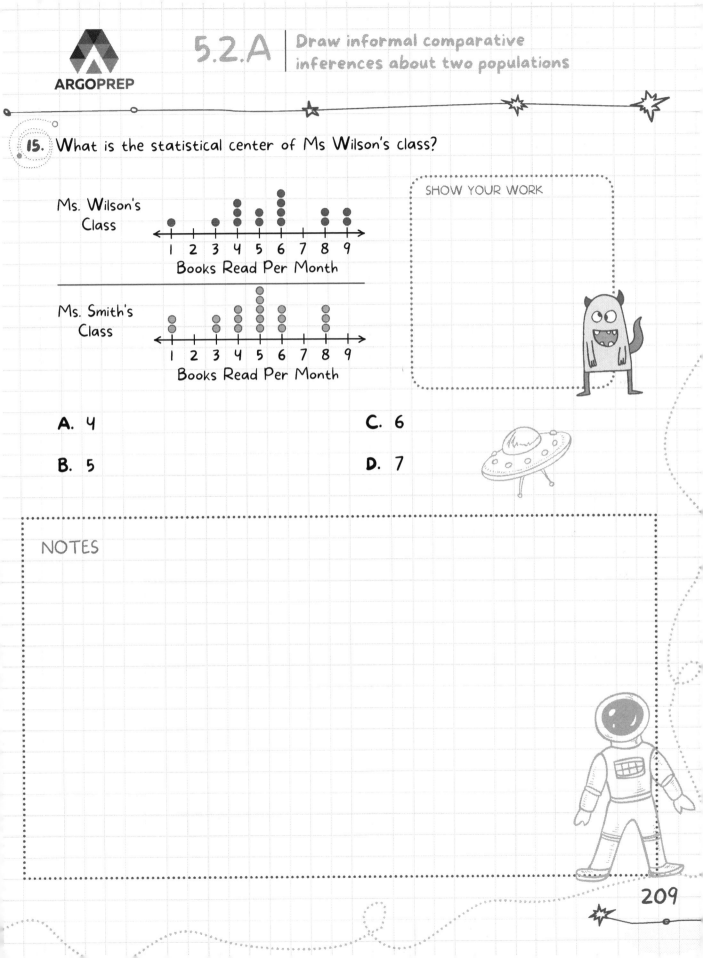

Books Read Per Month

Ms. Smith's Class

Books Read Per Month

SHOW YOUR WORK

A. 4

B. 5

C. 6

D. 7

NOTES

Let's look at some more statistical terms.

Mean: The average of the numbers

Median: The middle number in a data set

Mode: The number the occurs the most in a data set

Range: The spread of a data set from the highest to the lowest number

Let's apply these terms to a data set!

Justin and Micah are fishing. The weights of **5 fish** caught by each person are shown in this table.

Justin's Fish (oz.)	Micah's Fish (oz.)
24	19
20	15
18	14
24	40
30	13

Let's calculate! It's easiest to order the data from lowest to highest first:

13, 14, 15, 18, 19, 20, 24, 24, 30, 40

Mean: To calculate the mean, we add all the numbers together and then divide that result by the number of data points we have.

So, 13 + 14 + 15 + 18 + 19 + 20 + 24 + 24 + 30 + 40 = **217**

217 ÷ 10 = 21.7 is the statistical mean.

Median: To calculate the median, we determine, which number is in the middle. In this data set, the middle falls between **19** and **20**, so the median is **19.5** as we take the mean of the two numbers.

Mode: Which number occurs the most? There are **2 24s**, so the mode is **24**.

Range: The range is calculated by the highest number - the lowest number. The range is **40 - 13** or **27**.

1. What is the mode for this data set?

Lizzy and Yazmine are performing in a singing contest. This table shows the lengths of 4 songs they are preparing.

Lizzy's Songs (minutes)	Yazmine's Songs (minutes)
3.75	3.8
4	4.2
5.25	4
4.6	4.5

A. 1.5

B. 3.8

C. 4.2

D. 4

SHOW YOUR WORK

2. This table shows the average daily hours of sleep of 10 students in Zane's class and 10 students in Bryson's class.

Zane's Class	9	8	7	6	6	?	9	10	10	8
Bryson's Class	8	8	9	9	9	7	7	6	7	10

The range of Zane's data is greater than the range of Bryson's data. Which value is missing from Zane's data?

A. 10

B. 9

C. 5

D. 6

SHOW YOUR WORK

3. This table shows the average daily hours of sleep of 11 students in Gabriel's class and 11 students in Mario's class. What is the median of this data set?

Gabriel's Clas	6	7	8	8	10	11	7	7	9	8	10
Mario's Class	10	11	9	8	8	7	5	6	6	6	9

A. 8

B. 9

C. 10

D. 11

SHOW YOUR WORK

4. Alan is baking cookies. The values in this table list the amount of time it takes for each batch of cookies to bake.

	Alan's Cookies (minutes)
1st	25
2nd	25
3rd	22
4th	30
5th	?

SHOW YOUR WORK

The mean amount of time it takes for Alan's cookies to bake is **26** minutes. What is the missing time?

A. 26

B. 28

C. 30

D. 32

5. Sasha and Micah survey a random sample of **20** students to determine the amount of time it takes them to do their homework. Their results are as follows:
12, 12, 12, 16, 17, 19, 20, 24, 24, 26, 27, 29, 30, 34, 35, 36, 40, 41, 42, 63.
What is the mode of their data?

A. 27

B. 12

C. 51

D. 24

SHOW YOUR WORK

6. Sasha and Micah survey a random sample of **20** students to determine the amount of time it takes them to do their homework. Their results are as follows:
12, 12, 12, 16, 17, 19, 20, 24, 24, 26, 27, 29, 30, 34, 35, 36, 40, 41, 42, 63.
What is the range of their data?

A. 51

B. 12

C. 24

D. 26

SHOW YOUR WORK

7. Sasha and Micah survey a random sample of **20** students to determine the amount of time it takes them to do their homework. Their results are as follows:
12, 12, 12, 16, 17, 19, 20, 24, 24, 26, 27, 29, 30, 34, 35, 36, 40, 41, 42, 63.
What is the median of their data?

A. 20

B. 24

C. 25

D. 26.5

SHOW YOUR WORK

8. The scores for **2** math tests are graphed on the chart. What is the range of the chapter **2** test?

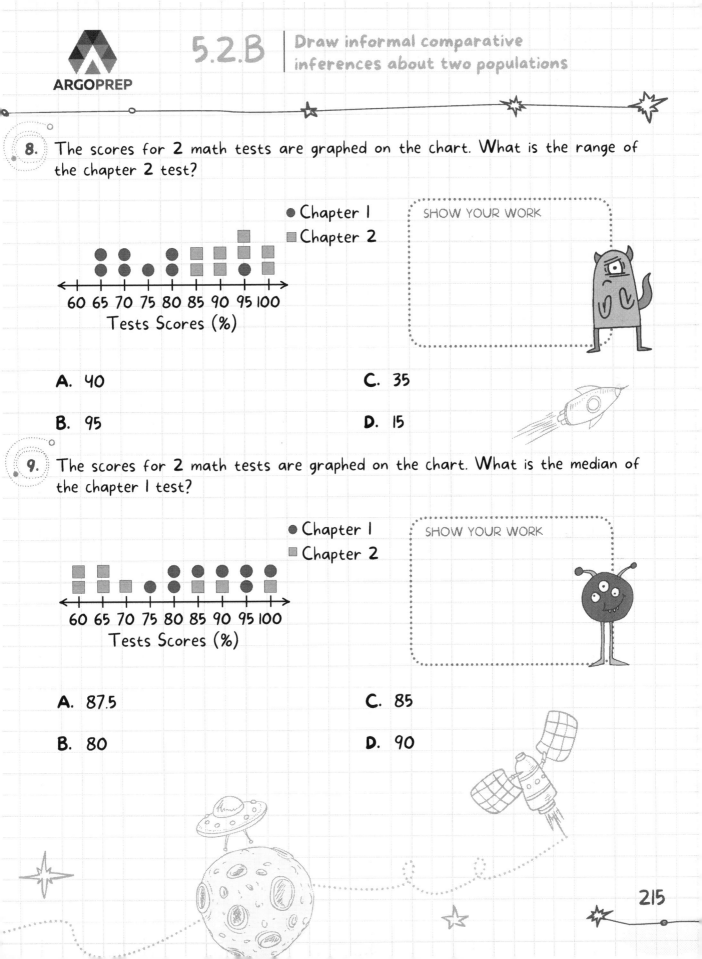

● Chapter 1
■ Chapter 2

SHOW YOUR WORK

60 65 70 75 80 85 90 95 100
Tests Scores (%)

A. 40

B. 95

C. 35

D. 15

9. The scores for **2** math tests are graphed on the chart. What is the median of the chapter 1 test?

● Chapter 1
■ Chapter 2

SHOW YOUR WORK

60 65 70 75 80 85 90 95 100
Tests Scores (%)

A. 87.5

B. 80

C. 85

D. 90

10. The scores for **2** math tests are graphed on the chart. What is the mean of both tests?

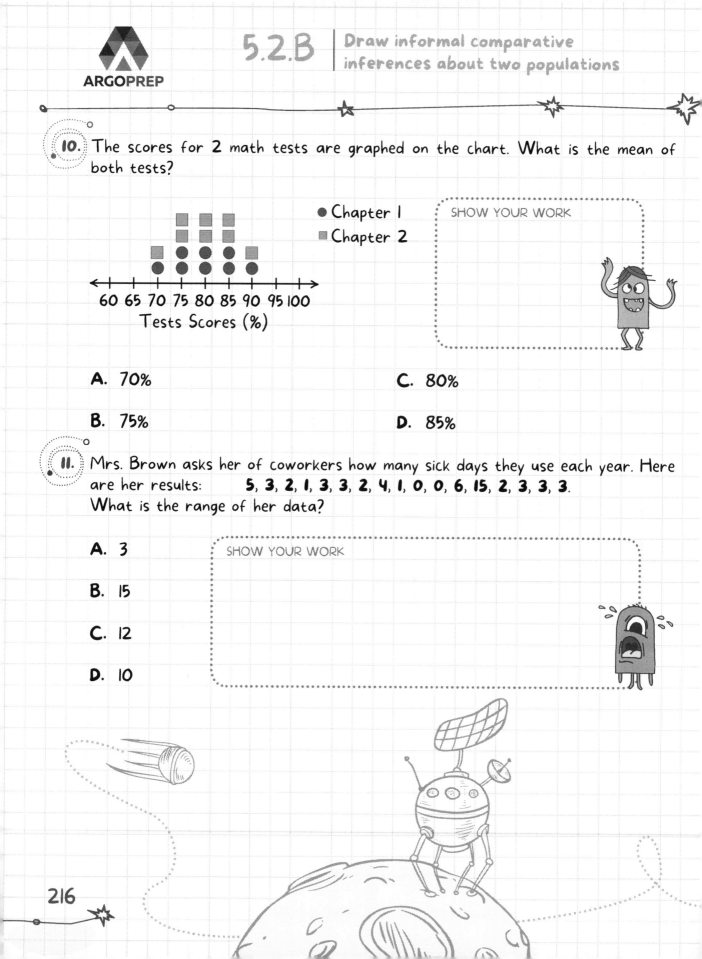

● Chapter 1
■ Chapter 2

60 65 70 75 80 85 90 95 100
Tests Scores (%)

SHOW YOUR WORK

A. 70%

C. 80%

B. 75%

D. 85%

11. Mrs. Brown asks her of coworkers how many sick days they use each year. Here are her results: **5, 3, 2, 1, 3, 3, 2, 4, 1, 0, 0, 6, 15, 2, 3, 3, 3.**
What is the range of her data?

A. 3

B. 15

C. 12

D. 10

SHOW YOUR WORK

12. Ava asks a group of seventh grade students how many pets they own. Here are her results: **0, 1, 2, 2, 3, 5, 2, 2, 1, 0, 1, 1, 2, 2, 3, 2.**
What is the median of her data?

A. 2

B. 1

C. 0

D. 3

SHOW YOUR WORK

13. Dara and David plan to determine the average length of the words in their Language Arts textbook. They took a random sample of 9 words from the first chapter. If the range was 10, what is one possible value for the missing figure?

Number of Letters (Chapter 1)	5	?	7	9	10	11	2	2	5

A. 9

B. 10

C. 11

D. 12

SHOW YOUR WORK

14. Cassandra and Nikki plan to determine the average length of the words in their Science textbook. They took a random sample of 8 words from the first chapter. If the mean word length for the first chapter is 8 letters, what is the missing value?

Number of Letters (Chapter 1)	?	9	6	7	12	11	10	5

A. 2

B. 3

C. 4

D. 5

SHOW YOUR WORK

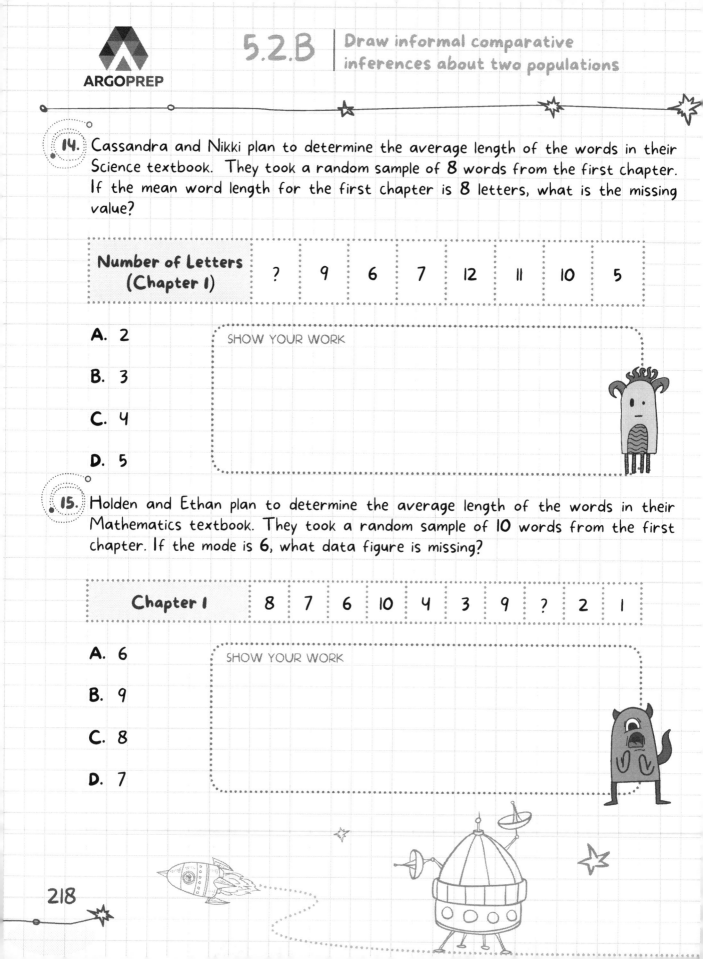

15. Holden and Ethan plan to determine the average length of the words in their Mathematics textbook. They took a random sample of 10 words from the first chapter. If the mode is 6, what data figure is missing?

Chapter 1	8	7	6	10	4	3	9	?	2	1

A. 6

B. 9

C. 8

D. 7

SHOW YOUR WORK

ARGOPREP

5.3.A | Investigate chance processes and develop, use, and evaluate probability models.

Do you know what probability is?

The probability of a chance event is a number between **0** and **1** that expresses the likelihood of an event occurring. **The larger the number, the greater the likelihood.** A probably near **0** is an **event that is unlikely** and the probability near 1 indicates a **likely event**.

Let's look at an example:

Joseph has a bag with **10 marble**s. The marbles are pink, blue, white, green and red. What is the probability of drawing a black marble from Joseph's bag?

It is impossible to draw a black marble because there are no black marbles in the bag.

There are **5 red marbles** and then **1 marble** of each other color. What is the probability of drawing a red marble?

The probability of drawing a red marble is greater than drawing any other color because there are more red marbles that any other color.

What is the probability of drawing a marble?

The probability of drawing a marble is certain because there are only marbles in the bag.

ARGOPREP

5.3.A | Investigate chance processes and develop, use, and evaluate probability models.

1. Larry has a bag with 15 marbles. There are 2 blue, 1 white, 6 black and 6 yellow marbles inside the bag. What is the probability of drawing a white marble from Larry's bag?

A. unlikely

B. impossible

C. neither unlikely or likely

D. certain

SHOW YOUR WORK

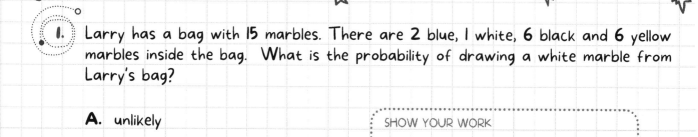

2. Kevin has a bag with 24 marbles. There are 15 red, 2 green, 2 black and 6 purple marbles inside the bag. What is the probability of drawing a pink marble from Kevin's bag?

A. unlikely

B. impossible

C. neither unlikely or likely

D. certain

SHOW YOUR WORK

3. Sarah is drawing marbles out of a bag. She determines the chances of selecting a red marble out of the bag is unlikely. Which response could describe the marbles in her bag?

A. 15 red marbles, 15 blue marbles

B. 30 blue marbles

C. 25 blue marbles, 5 red marbles

D. 25 red marbles, 5 blue marbles

SHOW YOUR WORK

ARGOPREP

5.3.A | Investigate chance processes and develop, use, and evaluate probability models.

4. Emerson is drawing marbles out of a bag. She determines the chances of selecting a black marble out of the bag is neither unlikely or likely. Which response could describe the marbles in his bag?

A. 45 black marbles, 15 white marbles

SHOW YOUR WORK

B. 60 white marbles

C. 60 black marbles

D. 30 black, 30 white marbles

5. Lucy is drawing marbles out of a bag. She determines the chances of selecting a white marble out of the bag is impossible. Which response could describe the marbles in her bag?

A. 45 black marbles, 15 white marbles

SHOW YOUR WORK

B. 60 white marbles

C. 60 black marbles

D. 30 black, 30 white marbles

ARGOPREP

5.3.A | Investigate chance processes and develop, use, and evaluate probability models.

6. The point shown on this number line represents the probability of an event.

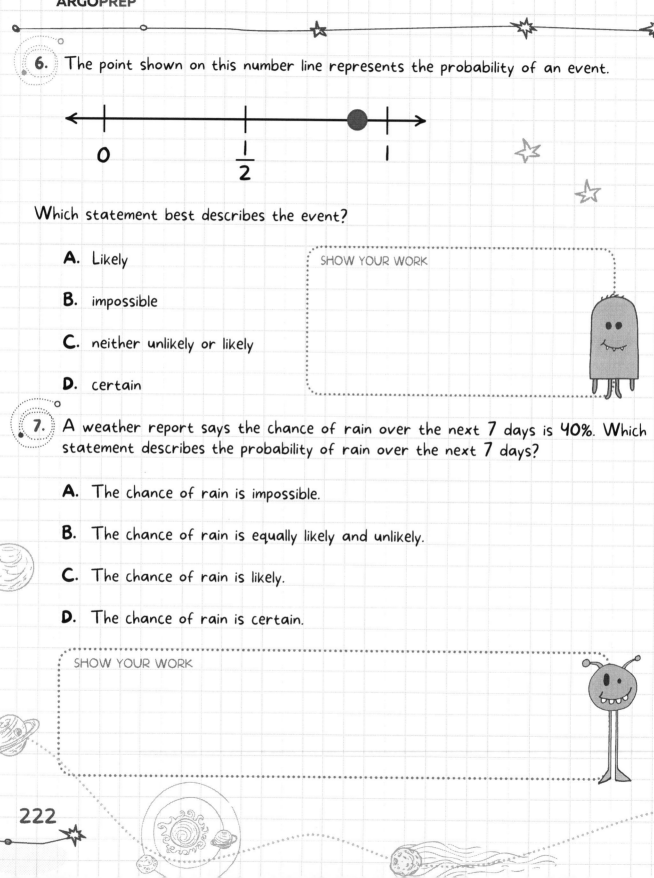

Which statement best describes the event?

A. Likely

B. impossible

C. neither unlikely or likely

D. certain

SHOW YOUR WORK

7. A weather report says the chance of rain over the next 7 days is 40%. Which statement describes the probability of rain over the next 7 days?

A. The chance of rain is impossible.

B. The chance of rain is equally likely and unlikely.

C. The chance of rain is likely.

D. The chance of rain is certain.

SHOW YOUR WORK

5.3.A | Investigate chance processes and develop, use, and evaluate probability models.

8. A weather report says the chance of rain over the next 7 days is 100%. Which statement describes the probability of rain over the next 7 days?

A. The chance of rain is impossible.

B. The chance of rain is equally likely and unlikely.

C. The chance of rain is likely.

D. The chance of rain is certain.

SHOW YOUR WORK

9. A weather report says the chance of rain over the next 7 days is 10%. Which statement describes the probability of rain over the next 7 days?

A. The chance of rain is impossible.

B. The chance of rain is equally likely and unlikely.

C. The chance of rain is likely.

D. The chance of rain is unlikely.

SHOW YOUR WORK

10. Kevin flips **3** coins. Each coin has **2** sides - heads and tails. What is the probability that the coins will land with at least **2** tails up?

A. unlikely

B. impossible

C. equally likely and unlikely

D. certain

SHOW YOUR WORK

11. Chandler flips **3** coins. Each coin has **2** sides - heads and tails. What is the probability that the coins will land with at least 1 tails up?

A. unlikely

B. likely

C. equally likely and unlikely

D. certain

SHOW YOUR WORK

12. Drea rolls a six-sided number cube. What is the probability she will land on a number greater than 1?

A. unlikely

B. likely

C. equally likely and unlikely

D. certain

SHOW YOUR WORK

ARGOPREP

5.3.A | Investigate chance processes and develop, use, and evaluate probability models.

13. A box contains 12 cards. Each card is marked with the numbers 1 through 12. What is the probability of drawing a card marked with an even number?

A. unlikely

B. likely

C. equally likely and unlikely

D. certain

SHOW YOUR WORK

14. Amanda has a spinner with 6 sections. Each section of the spinner is marked 1 through 6. What is the probability Amanda will spin and land on a number greater than 5?

A. unlikely

B. likely

C. equally likely and unlikely

D. certain

SHOW YOUR WORK

ARGOPREP

5.3.A | Investigate chance processes and develop, use, and evaluate probability models.

15. Natalia randomly draws a card from this set.

(2 x 4 + 1)	(7 x 2 - 3)
(8 ÷ 4 - 1)	(5 + 5 + 5)
(9 + 9 + 2)	(6 - 1 + 7)

What is the probability of selecting a card with an expression that is equivalent to an even number?

A. unlikely

B. likely

C. equally likely and unlikely

D. certain

SHOW YOUR WORK

NOTES

5.3.B | Investigate chance processes and develop, use, and evaluate probability models.

We can use what we know about situations to calculate probability.

We can actually calculate probability based on what we know about the potential outcomes. **To calculate the probability, we review the number of times a specific event can occur and divide it by the total number of events.**

There is a difference between theoretical and experimental probability. **Theoretical probability** is calculated based on the potential of an event. Experimental probability is calculated based on observation results of events that have happened.

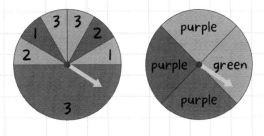

She spins both spinners at the same time. After 10 spins, these are her results:

(**1**, red), (**3**, green), (**3**, purple), (**1**, blue), (**2**, red)

(**2**, green), (1, blue), (**3**, purple), (**1**, red), (**2**, green)

What is the probability of rolling a **3**? It is likely because most of the circle is covered by **3**s. The **theoretical probability** of rolling a **3** is $\frac{8}{12}$ or 67%.

The experimental probability is $\frac{3}{10}$ or 30%.

What is the probability of rolling green?

The **theoretically probability** is $\frac{1}{4}$ or 25%.

The experimental probability is $\frac{3}{10}$ or 30%.

ARGOPREP

5.3.B | Investigate chance processes and develop, use, and evaluate probability models.

1. Lila rolls a six-sided number cube. The numbers on the cube are 1 through 6. Which value represents an accurate prediction of the number times the cube will land on **2** or **4**?

A. 33%

B. 66%

C. 50%

D. 75%

SHOW YOUR WORK

2. Issac surveys **24** students to determine their favorite animals. Of the students he surveyed, **8** said their favorite animal was cats. What is the experimental probability that the next student Issac talks to will say their favorite animal is cats?

A. 66%

B. 44%

C. 33%

D. 55%

SHOW YOUR WORK

3. Karla has a box of **150** pencils. Each time she draws a pencil from the box, she replaces it. After **60** draws, Karla selects **37** yellow pencils, and **23** black pencils. Which value is an accurate prediction of the number of black pencils inside Karla's box?

A. 90

B. 20

C. 125

D. 60

SHOW YOUR WORK

ARGOPREP

5.3.B | Investigate chance processes and develop, use, and evaluate probability models.

4. Tariq has a box of **80** pencils. Each time he draws a pencil from the box, he replaces it. After **20** draws, Tariq selects **8** white pencils, **2** blue pencils, and **10** green pencils. Which value is an accurate prediction of the number of blue pencils inside Tariq's box?

A. 1

B. 8

C. 18

D. 78

> SHOW YOUR WORK

5. Olivia has a box of **225** pencils. Each time she draws a pencil from the box, she replaces it. After **30** draws, Olivia selects **13** red pencils, **9** black pencils, and **8** green pencils. What is the experimental probability Olivia will select a red pencil on her next draw?

A. 23%

B. 43%

C. 63%

D. 83%

> SHOW YOUR WORK

6. Alex flips a coin. The coin has heads on one side, and tails on the other. Alex flips the coin **54** times. She lands on heads **22** times and tails **32** times. Which value is an accurate prediction of the number of times the coin will land on heads if it is flipped **80** times?

A. 50%

B. 20%

C. 75%

D. 100%

> SHOW YOUR WORK

ARGOPREP

5.3.B | Investigate chance processes and develop, use, and evaluate probability models.

7. Haley flips a coin, it has heads on one side, and tails on the other. Haley flips the coin **50** times. Which value is an accurate prediction of the number of times Haley should expect to have the coin land heads up?

A. 5

B. 10

C. 25

D. 45

SHOW YOUR WORK

8. Sarah is rolling a six-sided number cube **200** times. The numbers on the cube are the numbers 1-6. Which event is predicted to take place approximately **100** times?

A. Roll a six

B. Roll an even number

C. Roll a one

D. Roll a seven

SHOW YOUR WORK

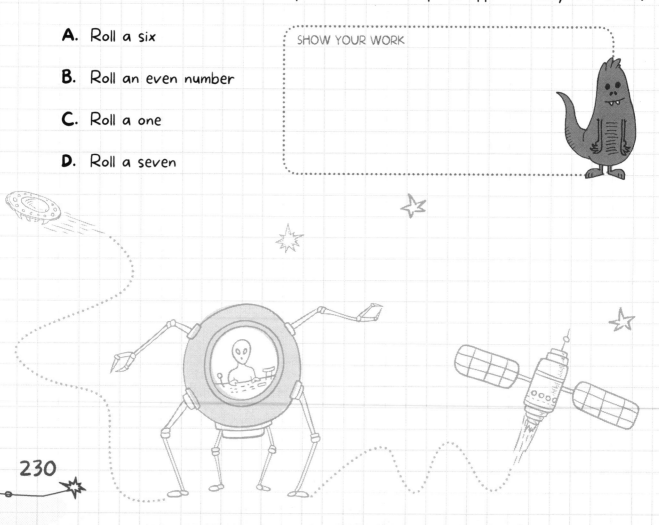

ARGOPREP

5.3.B | Investigate chance processes and develop, use, and evaluate probability models.

9. Nathaniel is rolling a six-sided number cube. The numbers on the cube are 10, 20, 30, 40, 50, and 60. He rolls the number cube 25 times. This table shows his results.

Number on Cube	Number of Rolls
10	卌
20	ⅢⅠ
30	Ⅲ
40	卌
50	Ⅲ
60	Ⅲ

SHOW YOUR WORK

What is the experimental probability the next number Nathaniel will roll is a 50?

A. 3%

B. 12%

C. 45%

D. 75%

10. Marion has a bag of marbles. She draws 12 blue marbles from the bag. If the bag contains 120 marbles, what is the experimental probability that the next marble Marion draws will be blue?

A. 85%

B. 65%

C. 35%

D. 10%

SHOW YOUR WORK

ARGOPREP

5.3.B | Investigate chance processes and develop, use, and evaluate probability models.

11. Vincent has a bag of marbles. He draws 14 yellow marbles from the bag. If the bag contains 50 marbles, what is the experimental probability the next marble Vincent draws out of the bag will be yellow?

A. 5%

B. 14%

C. 28%

D. 45%

SHOW YOUR WORK

12. Larissa has a bag of marbles. She draws 11 purple, 8 green, 10 red, and 10 blue marbles from the bag. If the bag contains 100 marbles, which value is a prediction of how many marbles are purple and green?

A. 51

B. 21

C. 35

D. 77

SHOW YOUR WORK

13. William is randomly drawing straws from a bag. He draws 2 straws that are 1-inch long, 7 straws that are 2-inches long, and 4 straws that are 3-inches long. What is the probability that he will draw another 1 inch straw?

A. 2%

B. 15%

C. 38%

D. 78%

SHOW YOUR WORK

5.3.B | Investigate chance processes and develop, use, and evaluate probability models.

14. Martin asks his friends which movie they like best. He surveys 16 friends, and 10 like Shrek. What is the experimental probability that the next friend Martin surveys will like Shrek?

A. 93%

B. 13%

C. 33%

D. 63%

SHOW YOUR WORK

15. The chance for snow over a 7-day period is **20%**. If the temperature and weather conditions remain the same, how many days will snowfall be predicted over a 21-day period?

A. 4

B. 8

C. 12

D. 18

SHOW YOUR WORK

NOTES

5.3.C | Investigate chance processes and develop, use, and evaluate probability models.

We can also calculate the probability of compound events. **A compound events means that two things are happening at once**. We can represent this by making a list.

What is the probability of flipping a coin and getting heads and rolling a 5?

There are **12 combination**s, TI, T2, T3, T4, T5, T6, HI, H2, H3, H4, H5, H6.

So the probability would be $\frac{1}{12}$ or 8%.

Another thing we calculate is statistics is events that are reliant on other events. These are called permutations and combinations. **A permutation is all the possible ways of doing something**. For example, say you have six friends and four of you are going to sit on a bench. For each seat of the bench, there is a different amount of people who can fit on a bench.

Seat 1: six people

Seat 2: five people

Seat 3: four people

To calculate the total number of possibilities we take **6 x 5 x 4** or **120** possibilities.

There is a formula for Permutations, involving factorials. Basically, a **factorial involves multiplying smaller factors together**. For example:

4! (4 factorial) is calculated by multiplying **4 x 3 x 2 x 1**

The Permutation formula is as follows:

If we have **n** items total and want to pick **k** in a certain order, we get:

$$P(n,k) = \frac{n!}{(n-k)!}$$

Combinations involve different possibilities but order does not matter. Let's say we are in a restaurant and want to order a pizza. There are **15** possible toppings and we want to order **3**. How many possible combinations of toppings are there?

There is a formula for combinations too! The number of ways to combine **k** items from a set of **n** is

$$C(n,k) = \frac{n!}{(n-k)!\,k!}$$

Using our topping example, we would take **15!** divided by **(15 - 3)! × 3!**

Using that formula, we got an answer of **455** different combinations.

NOTES

ARGOPREP

5.3.C | Investigate chance processes and develop, use, and evaluate probability models.

1. There are 12 students auditioning for 3 parts in the school play. How many permutations of students are possible?

A. 220

B. 330

C. 1,320

D. 830

SHOW YOUR WORK

2. Mrs. Johnson wants to organize 5-person teams for an upcoming project. There are 19 students in Mrs. Johnson's class. Which expression represents the number of possible combinations?

A. $19! \div 14!$

B. $19! \div 5!$

C. $19! \div (14! \times 5!)$

D. $14!$

SHOW YOUR WORK

3. Nathan rolls two number cubes labeled with the numbers 1-6. Rolling each number cube is an independent event. What is the probability Nathan will roll an even number on the first cube and a five on the second cube?

A. $\frac{1}{3}$

B. $\frac{1}{6}$

C. $\frac{1}{2}$

D. $\frac{1}{12}$

SHOW YOUR WORK

ARGOPREP

5.3.C | Investigate chance processes and develop, use, and evaluate probability models.

4. Lila's mother is catering a birthday party. She provides fish or chicken as the main entrée and offers the guests 3 different side vegetables.
This table shows the meal selections of the first 45 people who attend the party.

	Salad	Rice	Squash
Fish	7	9	5
Chicken	7	8	9

Based on these results, what is the experimental probability that the next person will order a fish dinner with squash?

A. 6%

B. 11%

C. 66%

D. 15%

SHOW YOUR WORK

5. Luis and his family are deciding which movies to see this month. They plan to see one movie each weekend for 4 weeks. Luis writes down the names of 7 movies, each on a separate piece of paper. He then places the pieces of paper in a jar for his family members to select 4 movies at random.
How many movie permutations are possible?

A. 220

B. 840

C. 1260

D. 4

SHOW YOUR WORK

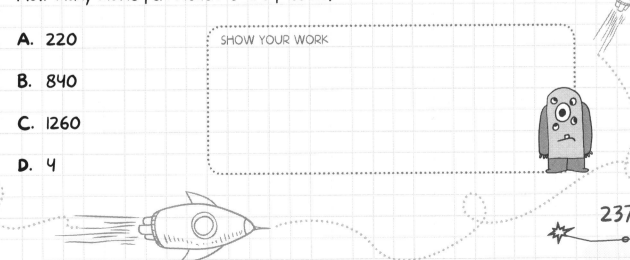

5.3.C | Investigate chance processes and develop, use, and evaluate probability models.

ARGOPREP

6. Murphy chooses a shirt, a pair of pants, and a pair of socks to wear to school each day. This table lists the color of each piece of clothing.

Shirt	Pants	Socks
White	Blue	White
Black	Khaki	Black
Red	Black	Tan

SHOW YOUR WORK

What is the probability that Murphy will wear black pants?

A. $\frac{1}{9}$

B. $\frac{1}{27}$

C. $\frac{1}{3}$

D. $\frac{6}{15}$

7. Elijah chooses a combination of a snack and drink each day after school. The snacks include popcorn, chips, and fruit. The drinks include juice, milk, and water.

popcorn — juice
        — milk
        — water

chips — juice
      — milk
      — water

fruit — juice
      — milk
      — water

SHOW YOUR WORK

What is the probability that Elijah will choose popcorn with juice?

A. $\frac{1}{9}$

B. $\frac{1}{3}$

C. $\frac{4}{6}$

D. $\frac{5}{7}$

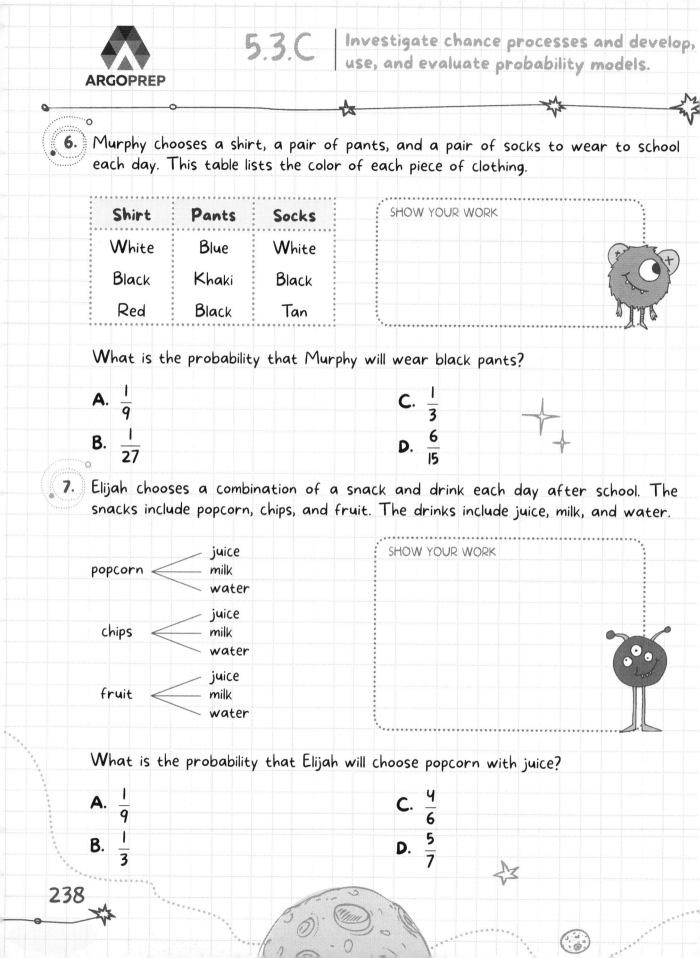

ARGOPREP

5.3.C | Investigate chance processes and develop, use, and evaluate probability models.

8. A sports magazine is featuring 4 different athletes in the next issue. In how many different orders could the athletes be featured?

A. 10

B. 24

C. 76

D. 120

SHOW YOUR WORK

9. Natalie and her friends are making cookies. They need to add flour, white sugar, brown sugar, baking powder, and eggs to a bowl. In how many different orders can Natalie these ingredients be added?

A. $\frac{1}{6}$

B. 6

C. 120

D. 355

SHOW YOUR WORK

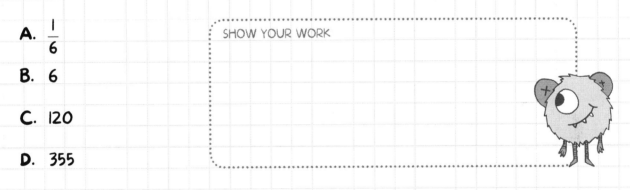

ARGOPREP

5.3.C | Investigate chance processes and develop, use, and evaluate probability models.

10. A restaurant creates pizza using these ingredients.

Crust	Meat	Sauce	Vegetable
Regular Thin Pan-Style	Sausage Pepperoni Hamburger Bacon	Tomato Ranch BBQ	Onion Mushroom Tomato Bell Pepper Olive

How many different combinations of pizzas can this restaurant prepare if you can select only one item from each category?

SHOW YOUR WORK

A. 2,402

B. 360

C. 180

D. 15

11. Mr. Jones is arranging the items on his bookshelf. He has a spiral notebook, a mathematics text book and a teaching award. In how many different orders can he arrange these items?

SHOW YOUR WORK

A. 9

B. 6

C. 12

D. 4

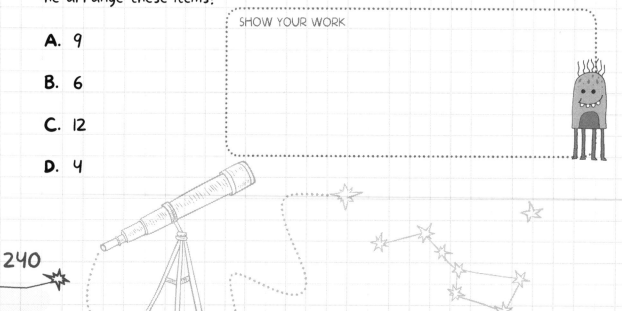

ARGOPREP

5.3.C | Investigate chance processes and develop, use, and evaluate probability models.

12. A jar contains **2** red beads, **6** green beads and **2** blue beads. What is the probability of selecting a blue bead, replacing it, and then selecting a green bead?

A. 80%

B. 60%

C. 20%

D. 12%

SHOW YOUR WORK

13. The numbers 1 through 10 are written on a card and placed in a bowl. A card is drawn at random then replaced after being drawn. What is the probability of drawing the number 10 and then a number greater than 5?

A. $\frac{1}{20}$

B. $\frac{1}{10}$

C. $\frac{5}{10}$

D. $\frac{3}{10}$

SHOW YOUR WORK

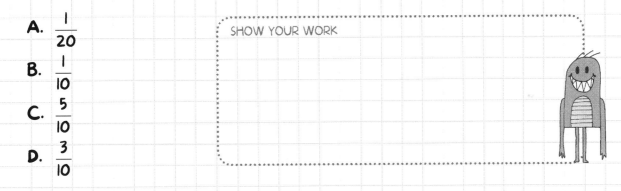

14. Karen chooses a shirt, a pair of pants, and a pair of socks to wear to school each day. This table lists the color of each piece of clothing.

Shirt	Pants	Socks
White	Blue	White
Red	Black	Black
		Tan

Make a list to represent the total number of possible combinations.

SHOW YOUR WORK

15. The letters that form the word TENNESSEE are placed in a bowl. How would you determine the probability of choosing a consonant letter, replacing it and then drawing a "S"?

SHOW YOUR WORK

1. Marquis is preparing to fly from Honolulu to Seattle. There are 150 passengers on the flight. Marquis determines 16% of the passengers are children. Which response describes a random sample Marquis could have used to make this prediction?

A. Marquis counted the number of children in the first 10 rows of the plane.

B. Marquis asked the person sitting next to him to predict how many passengers are children.

C. Marquis asked the 4 flight attendants how many of the passengers are children.

D. Marquis counts the number of seats on the plane.

SHOW YOUR WORK

2. Alex places 100 marbles inside a bag. The marbles are blue, black, green and red. After drawing a marble out of the bag 20 times, he takes out 9 black marbles, 4 blue marbles, 5 red marbles, and 2 green marbles. Based on his sample, about how many marbles in the bag are green?

A. 80

B. 20

SHOW YOUR WORK

C. 2

D. 10

3. Ben collects data about a group of travelers' recent visit to Puerto Rico. He records his data in this table.

Level of Satisfaction with Visit	Number of People
1 - Unsatisfied	1
2 - Somewhat satisfied	2
3 - Satisfied	5
4 - Very satisfied	4

What is a conclusion Ben can draw based on his data?

A. The majority of people were unsatisfied with their trip.

B. The majority of people were satisfied with their trip.

C. All people were unsatisfied about the trip.

D. The majority of people were undecided about their trip.

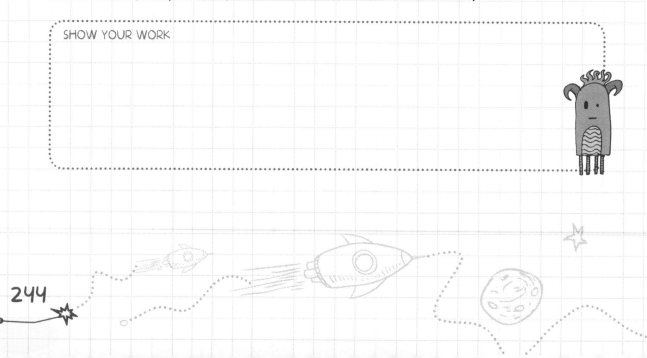

SHOW YOUR WORK

4. The data in this bar graph shows the different sports played by the students in Bryson's class.

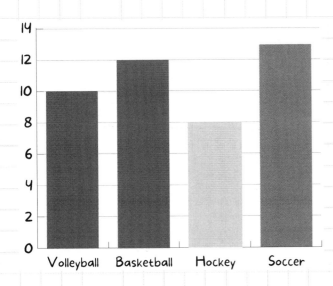

There are **575** students in Bryson's school. Using this data to make inferences about the entire school, how many students play hockey?

A. 55

B. 426

C. 110

D. 260

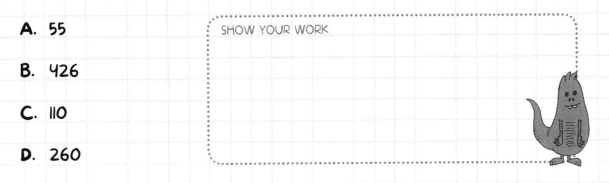

SHOW YOUR WORK

5. What is the statistical center of Mrs Smith's class?

Ms. Smith's Class

Books Read Per Month
1 2 3 4 5 6 7 8 9

Ms. Dhabi's Class

Books Read Per Month
1 2 3 4 5 6 7 8 9

SHOW YOUR WORK

A. 1

C. 3

B. 2

D. 4

6. What is the statistical distribution of Ms. Dhabi's class?

Ms. Smith's Class

Books Read Per Month
1 2 3 4 5 6 7 8 9

Ms. Dhabi's Class

Books Read Per Month
1 2 3 4 5 6 7 8 9

SHOW YOUR WORK

A. 9

C. 7

B. 8

D. 6

7. Harriet is baking cookies. The values in this table list the amount of time it takes for each batch of cookies to bake. The batches take **?, 26, 29, 28** and **26** minutes. The mean for the batch is **27** minutes. How long did the first batch take?

	Harriet's Cookies (minutes)
1st	?
2nd	26
3rd	29
4th	28
5th	26

A. 26 minutes

B. 27 minutes

C. 28 minutes

D. 29 minutes

SHOW YOUR WORK

8. Jonathan surveys a random sample of 13 students at his school to find out how many students ride the bus. Four students ride the bus. Which number is an appropriate prediction of the number of students in the school who ride the bus if there are 175 students at his school?

A. 4

B. 14

C. 54

D. 114

SHOW YOUR WORK

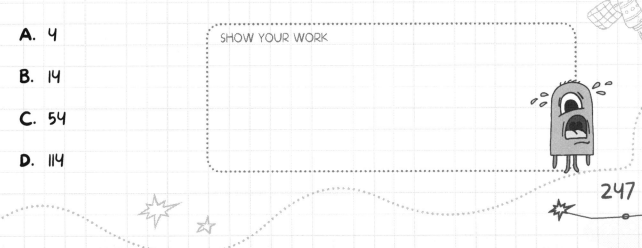

9. Larson has a bag with 15 marbles. There are 2 blue, 1 white, 6 black and 6 yellow marbles inside the bag. What is the probability of drawing a white marble from Larson's bag?

  A. unlikely

  B. impossible

  C. neither unlikely or likely

  D. certain

SHOW YOUR WORK

10. The point shown on this number line represents the probability of an event.

$$\xleftarrow{\qquad | \qquad \bullet \qquad | \qquad} \longrightarrow$$

0      $\frac{1}{2}$ 1

Which statement best describes the event?

  A. The event is likely to happen.

  B. The event is certain to happen.

  C. The event is impossible.

  D. The event is as unlikely to happen as it is likely to happen.

SHOW YOUR WORK

11. Earl flips a coin. The coin has heads on one side, and tails on the other. Earl flips the coin **500** times. Which value is an accurate prediction of the number of times Earl should expect the coin to land on heads?

A. 100

B. 215

C. 250

D. 375

SHOW YOUR WORK

12. Myles is rolling a six-sided number cube **300** times. The numbers on the cube are the numbers 1-6. Which event is predicted to take place approximately **200** times?

A. Rolling 1-4

B. Rolling an even number

C. Rolling a 1

D. Rolling 2 or 3

SHOW YOUR WORK

13. Mark rolls two dice 10 times. He observes $\frac{5}{10}$ of his rolls resulted in at least one five. Mark combines his results with the other students in his class and discovers $\frac{11}{40}$ of the rolls for the entire class resulted in at least one five.

How do the results of Mark's class compare to the fraction of possible outcomes for rolling at least one five?

A. They are unrelated.

B. Equal to the possible outcomes

C. Higher than the possible outcomes

D. Lower than the possible outcomes

SHOW YOUR WORK

14. A number cube contains the numbers 1 through 6. Which probability model represents the chance of rolling an odd number on this number cube?

A. $\frac{5}{6}$

B. $\frac{2}{6}$

C. $\frac{1}{6}$

D. $\frac{1}{2}$

SHOW YOUR WORK

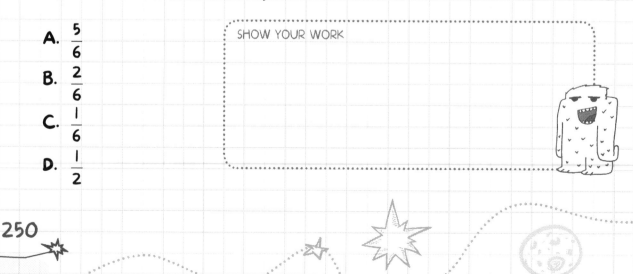

15. Roberta flips 3 coins. She records the possibilities of flipping each coin heads up, H, and tails up, T, in a list. Each coin flip is an independent event.
What is the probability of getting 3 heads?

A. $\dfrac{1}{2}$

B. $\dfrac{1}{8}$

C. $\dfrac{2}{4}$

D. $\dfrac{3}{6}$

SHOW YOUR WORK

16. Donna chooses a shirt, a pair of pants, and a pair of socks to wear to school each day. This table lists the color of each piece of clothing.

Shirt	Pants	Socks
White	Blue	White
Black	Khaki	Black
	Black	Tan

What is the probability that Donna will wear khaki pants?

A. $\dfrac{1}{8}$

B. $\dfrac{1}{6}$

C. $\dfrac{1}{3}$

D. $\dfrac{3}{9}$

SHOW YOUR WORK

ARGOPREP

17. Christopher watches one of his **3** favorite television shows in the morning, and one of his **4** favorite television shows in the afternoon.

Morning Television Shows	Afternoon Television Shows
The Cartoon Hour	The Adventures of Zedd
Kit and Kaboodle	Agents of I.M.A.G.E.
Thunder Birds	The Animal Show
	Keith and Eddie

How many different combinations are possible?

A. 12

B. 7

C. 8

D. 15

SHOW YOUR WORK

18. A drink machine offers water, iced tea, milk and juice. How many ways can these drinks be arranged in the machine?

A. 6

B. 18

C. 12

D. 24

SHOW YOUR WORK

19. A jar contains 4 red beads, 7 green beads and 9 blue beads. What is the probability of selecting a red bead, replacing it, and then selecting a blue bead?

A. 20%

B. 16%

C. 9%

D. 6%

SHOW YOUR WORK

20. A veterinarian is developing the patient schedule for next week. There are 5 animals to be added to the schedule. In how many different orders could the animals be added to the schedule?

A. 13

B. 120

C. 150

D. 200

SHOW YOUR WORK

Chapter 6 :
Mixed Assessment

ARGOPREP

ARGOPREP

1. A store is selling **60** apples for **$45**. What is the unit rate?

A. $1.00

B. $1.25

SHOW YOUR WORK

C. $0.50

D. $0.75

2. Graham runs **4** miles in an hour. How long does it take him to run 1 mile?

A. 4 minutes

B. 15 minutes

SHOW YOUR WORK

C. 45 minutes

D. 0.25 minutes

3. Which ratio is **6:18** lowest form?

A. 1:3

SHOW YOUR WORK

B. 3:1

C. 12:36

D. 12:4

4. Which ratio is equal to $\frac{1}{8}$?

   A. 6 to 48

   B. 32 to 4

   C. $\frac{72}{9}$

   D. 5:12

   SHOW YOUR WORK

5. If a gallon of paint covers $\frac{2}{3}$ of a wall, how many gallons will it take to cover all of the room's 4 walls?

   A. 3 gallons

   B. 4 gallons

   C. 6 gallons

   D. 7 gallons

   SHOW YOUR WORK

6. Luis walks to school and home every day. The walk is $\frac{3}{4}$ miles. It takes him 15 minutes. If he walks the same pace, how far does he walk in a hour?

   A. 2 miles

   B. 3 miles

   C. 4 miles

   D. 5 miles

   SHOW YOUR WORK

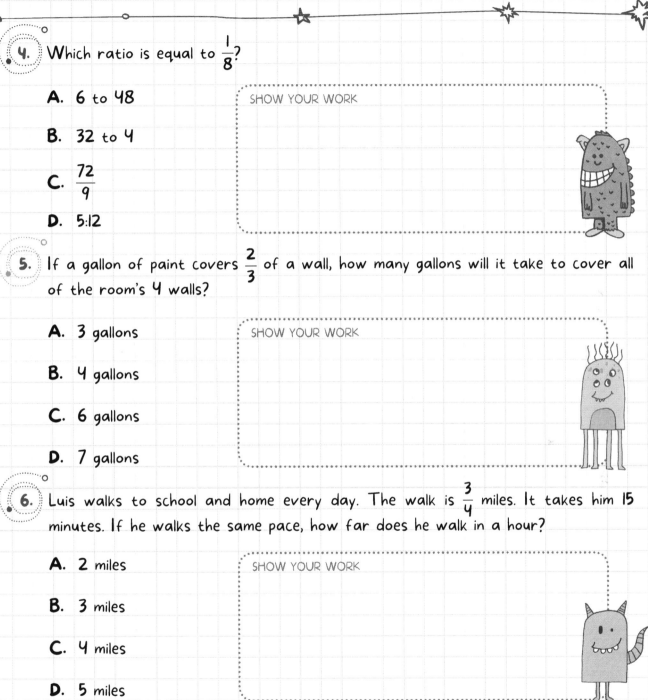

7. Which answer would be a correct value for y in the equation $x = \frac{1}{2}y$ if $x = 30$?

   A. 15

   B. 30

   C. 45

   D. 60

   SHOW YOUR WORK

8. Which answer would be a correct value for x in the equation $x = 20y$ if $y = \frac{1}{4}$?

   A. 5

   B. 4

   C. 3

   D. 2

   SHOW YOUR WORK

9. What is the constant rate for these values?

   (2, 3) (4, 6) (6, 9)

   A. $\frac{2}{3}$

   B. $\frac{3}{2}$

   C. +2

   D. +3

   SHOW YOUR WORK

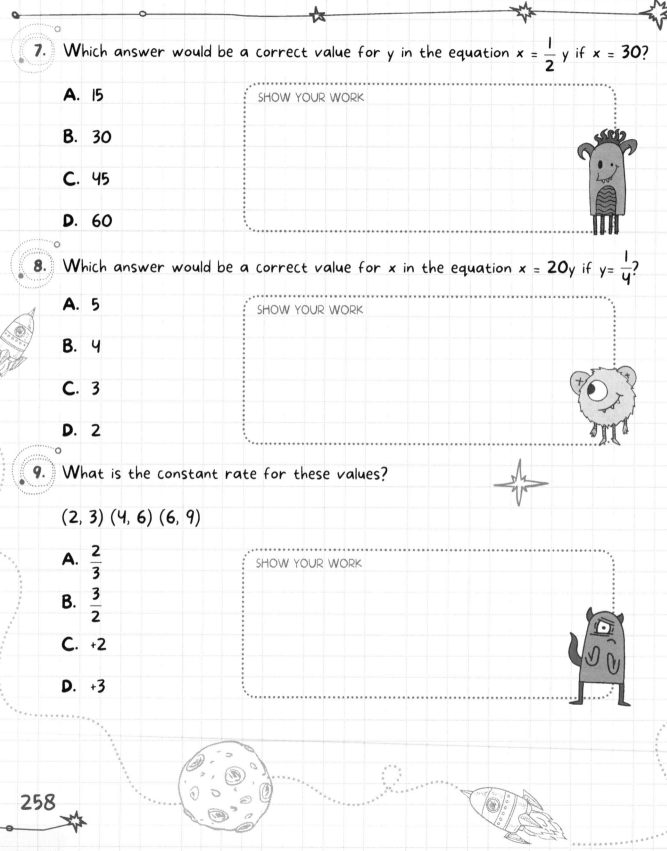

10. What is the constant rate for these values?

x	y
1	3
3	9
5	15

A. 3

B. $\dfrac{1}{3}$

C. 6

D. $\dfrac{2}{5}$

SHOW YOUR WORK

11. If the relationship is represented by the equation $y = 4x$, and $x = 4$, what is y?

A. 1

B. 12

C. 16

D. 20

SHOW YOUR WORK

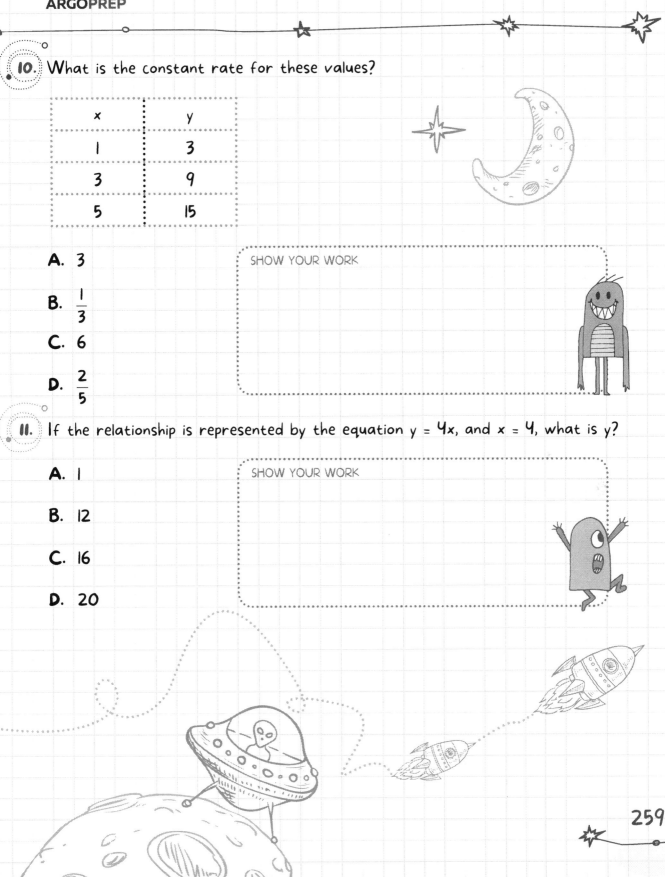

12. If you were to graph the line y = 10x, which point would fall on the line?

A. (50, 15)

B. (5, 6)

C. (20, 2)

D. (3, 30)

SHOW YOUR WORK

13. If you were to graph the line y = 15x, which point would fall on the line?

A. (7, 8)

B. (3, 5)

C. (4, 60)

D. (45, 3)

SHOW YOUR WORK

14. If you were to graph the line y = $\frac{1}{2}$x, which point would fall on the line?

A. (5, 10)

B. (8, 16)

C. (32, 16)

D. (8, 3)

SHOW YOUR WORK

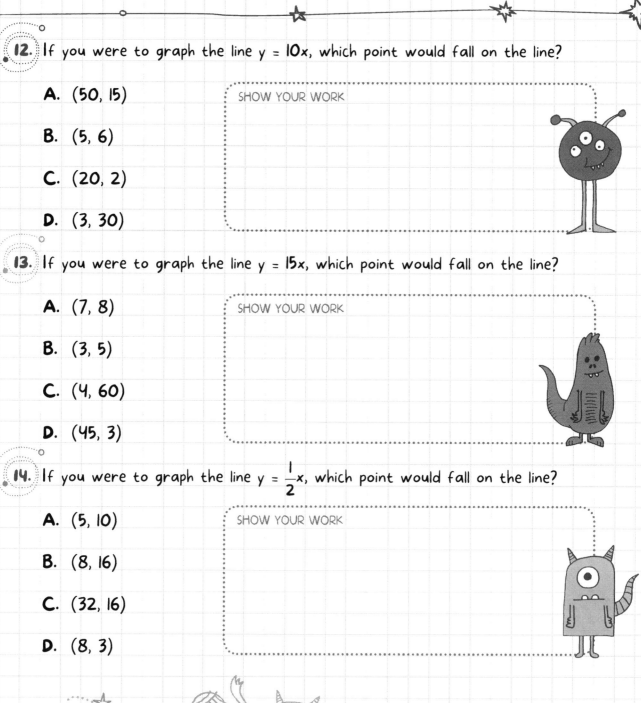

15. Max sells a house for **$120,000**. He makes a **3%** commission. How much money will he make on the sale?

A. $3,600

B. $116, 400

C. $7,200

D. $1, 200

SHOW YOUR WORK

16. Sam buys **$78** worth of groceries. He has to pay **5%** tax on his purchase. He has **$82**. Does he have enough money to make his purchase? Explain your response.

SHOW YOUR WORK

17. A store adds some items to its shelf and increases their original cost due to high demand by **15%**. Sherrie is interested in buying a rug that was originally priced at **$325**. What is the new price of the item?

A. $48.75

B. $373.75

C. $340

D. $305

SHOW YOUR WORK

18. Marisa and her mom go out to lunch and their bill is $22. If they want to tip their waitress the standard 15%, what will the total amount of their bill be?

A. $23.20

B. $25.50

C. $25.30

D. $27.20

SHOW YOUR WORK

19. The number of students in 7th grade went from 220 last year to 250 this year. What was the percent increase?

A. 14%

B. 15%

C. 88%

D. 85%

SHOW YOUR WORK

20. Lucas took a math test and got $\frac{15}{22}$ questions right. What was his percent error?

A. 32%

B. 68%

C. 15%

D. 22%

SHOW YOUR WORK

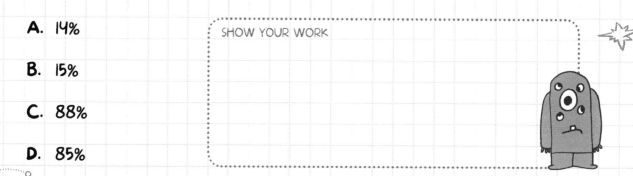

21. What number can be added to -122 to make a sum of 0?

A. 112

B. 0

C. -122

D. 122

SHOW YOUR WORK

22. -32 + -46

A. -14

B. 78

C. -78

D. 14

SHOW YOUR WORK

23. 37 + -45

A. -72

B. 72

C. -8

D. 8

SHOW YOUR WORK

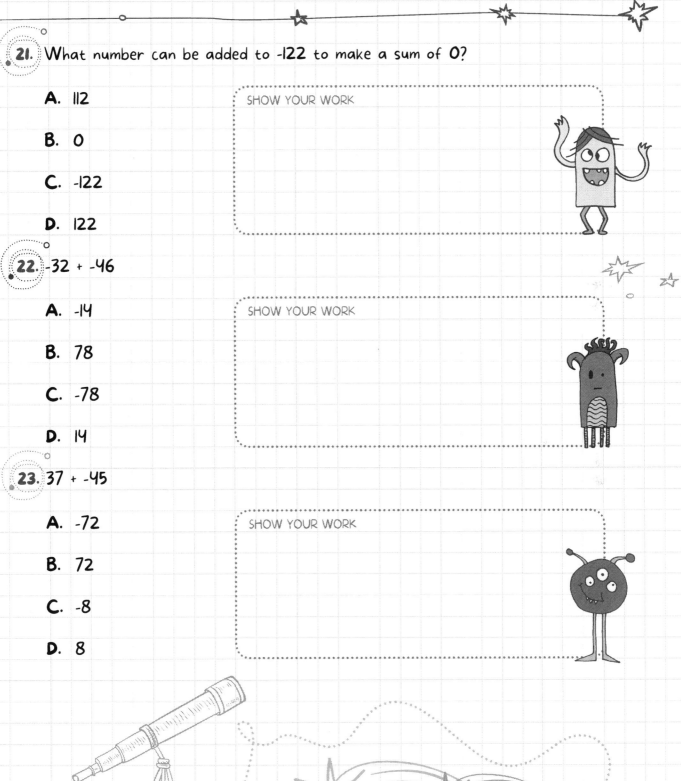

24. -32 + 69

A. -37

B. 37

C. 101

D. -101

SHOW YOUR WORK

25. 72 - -29

A. 43

B. 101

C. -101

D. -43

SHOW YOUR WORK

26. -39 - 82

A. -121

B. 43

C. 121

D. 43

SHOW YOUR WORK

27. -39 - -24

A. 63

B. -63

C. -15

D. 15

SHOW YOUR WORK

28. -14 × 45

A. -630

B. 630

C. 315

D. D. 5

SHOW YOUR WORK

29. -13 × -92

A. -1,172

B. 1,170

C. -1,196

D. 1,196

SHOW YOUR WORK

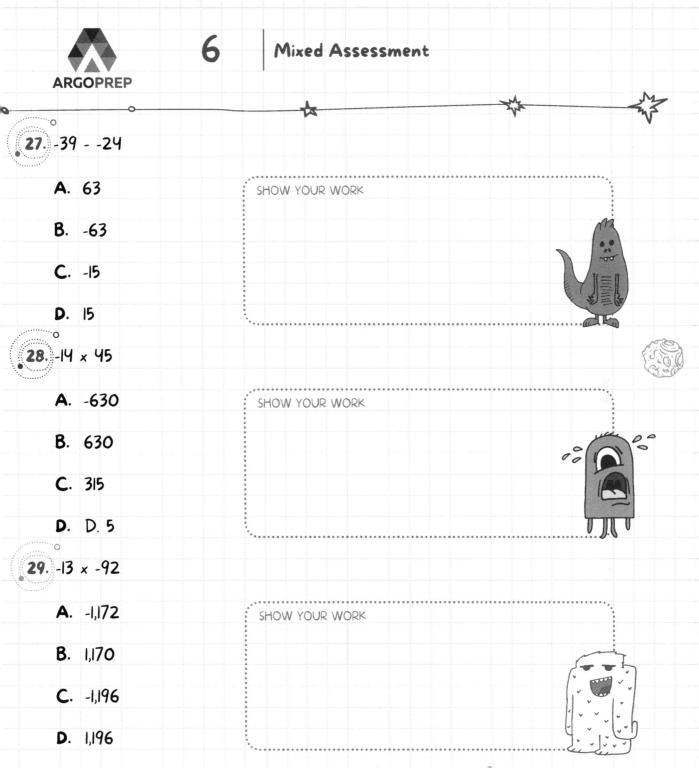

30. 63 × -20

   A. -1,500

   B. -1,000

   C. -1,260

   D. 1, 260

SHOW YOUR WORK

31. 168 ÷ -14

   A. -12

   B. 12

   C. 13

   D. -14

SHOW YOUR WORK

32. -434 ÷ -7

   A. -62

   B. 62

   C. 61

   D. -60

SHOW YOUR WORK

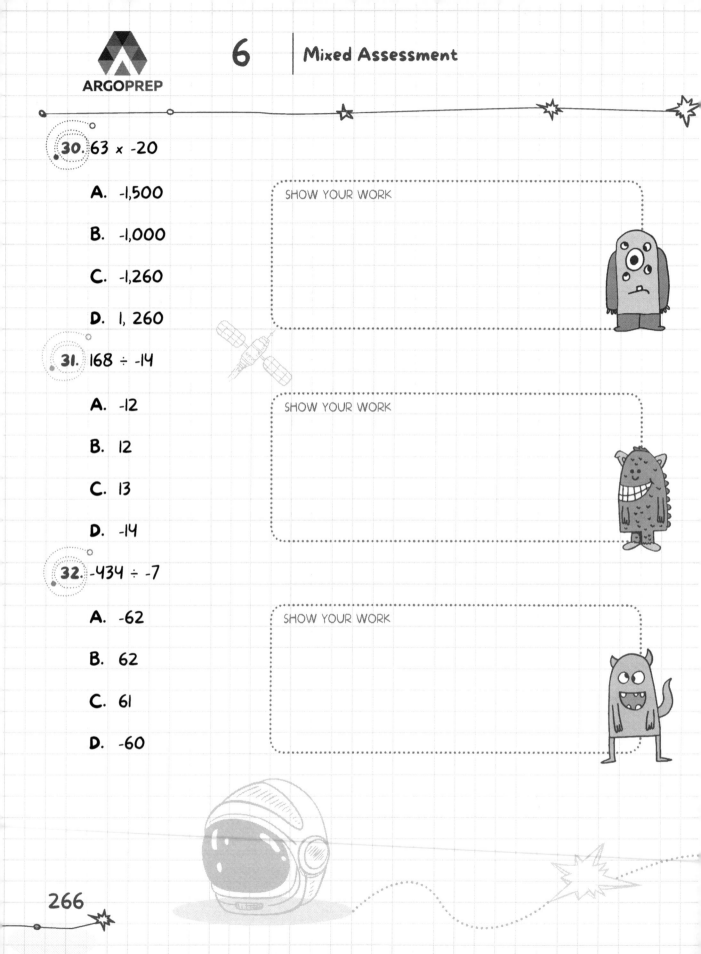

33. -805 ÷ 23

A. -35

B. 35

C. -32

D. 37

SHOW YOUR WORK

34. Represent -6 + -4 on a number line.

SHOW YOUR WORK

35. Represent -4 +5 on a number line.

SHOW YOUR WORK

36. Yesterday, the temperature outside was -12. Today, the temperature was 15 degrees warmer. What was the temperature today?

A. -3

B. -27

C. 3

D. 15

SHOW YOUR WORK

37. Last week, the average temperature was -7. This week, the average temperature is 11 degrees colder. What was the average temperature this week?

A. 18

B. -18

C. -5

D. 5

SHOW YOUR WORK

38. A diver was diving in the ocean. She started at a depth of -5 feet and dove 15 more feet. What was her new depth level?

A. 0

B. -5

C. 20

D. -20

SHOW YOUR WORK

39. A diver was working in the ocean. She started at -28 feet and rose 15 feet. What was her new sea level?

A. -13

B. -15

C. 13

D. 15

SHOW YOUR WORK

40. A hiker was going along a trail. He went up 150 feet, down 225 feet and up 130. What was his final position if he started at sea level?

A. 55

B. -55

C. -35

D. 35

SHOW YOUR WORK

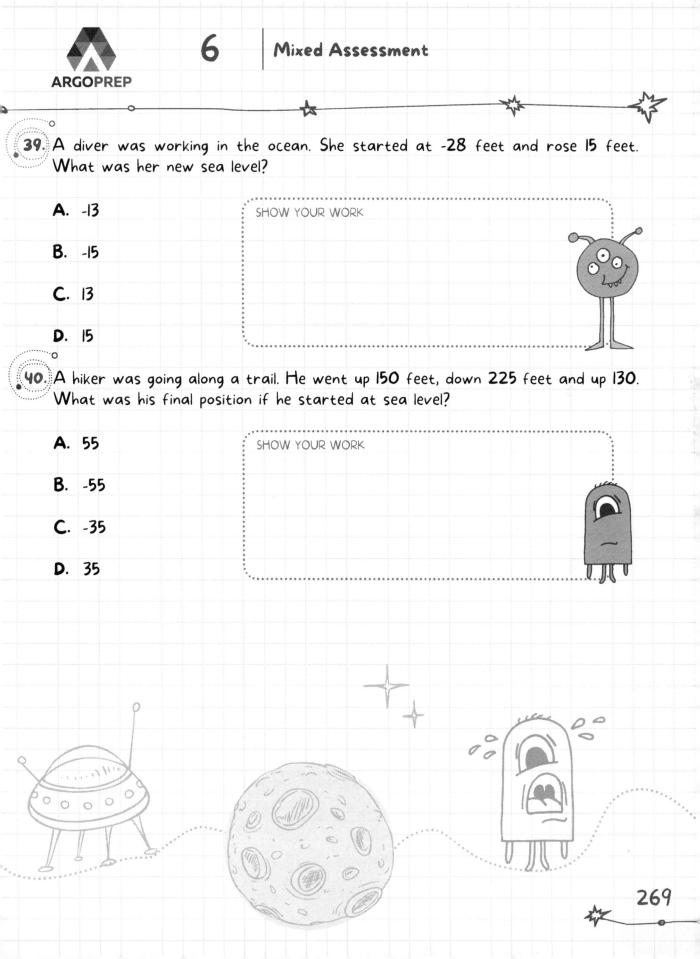

41. Simplify the expression 18x - 32 if x = 4

    A. 40

    B. 10

    C. 4

    D. 1

SHOW YOUR WORK

42. Factor the expression $14a^2 + 7a$

    A. 7(2a + 1)

    B. a(7a + 1)

    C. 7a(2a + 1)

    D. $7a^2 (a + 1)$

SHOW YOUR WORK

43. Distribute to simplify. 5(2n + 3m - 9)

    A. -15n

    B. n + 15m - 15

    C. 10n + 14m - 45

    D. 10n + 15m - 45

SHOW YOUR WORK

44. Which expression is equal to the product of a number and 15?

A. 15 + n

B. 15n

C. n + 15

D. n - 15

SHOW YOUR WORK

45. Which expression is equal to twelve less than twice a number?

A. 2n - 12

B. 12n - 2

C. 12(n - 2)

D. 2(n - 12)

SHOW YOUR WORK

46. Which expression is equal to three more than a number cubed?

A. $n^3 - 3$

B. $3n^3$

C. $n^3 + 3$

D. $3n^3 + 3$

SHOW YOUR WORK

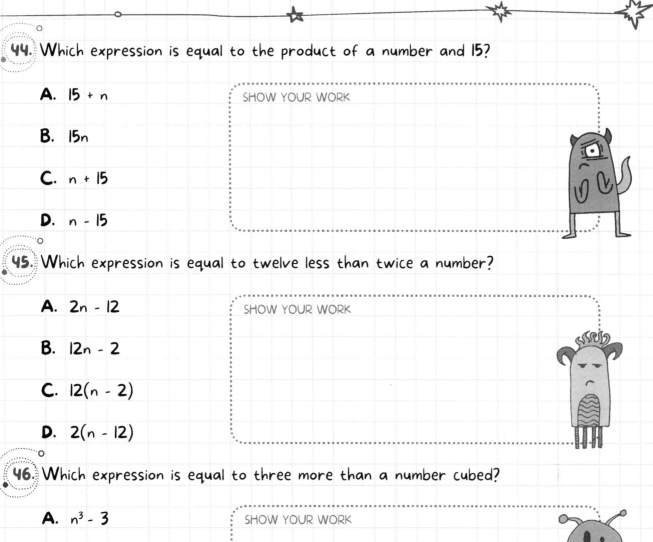

47. A garden has a length of 4. Write an expression that illustrates its perimeter.

A. 2w + 2

B. 4w

C. 2w + 8

D. 8w

SHOW YOUR WORK

48. $\frac{1}{3}$ + 1.75

A. 2.083

B. 2.380

C. 2.375

D. 2.573

SHOW YOUR WORK

49. 0.8 × $\frac{3}{4}$

A. $\frac{1}{5}$

B. $\frac{4}{5}$

C. $\frac{2}{5}$

D. $\frac{3}{5}$

SHOW YOUR WORK

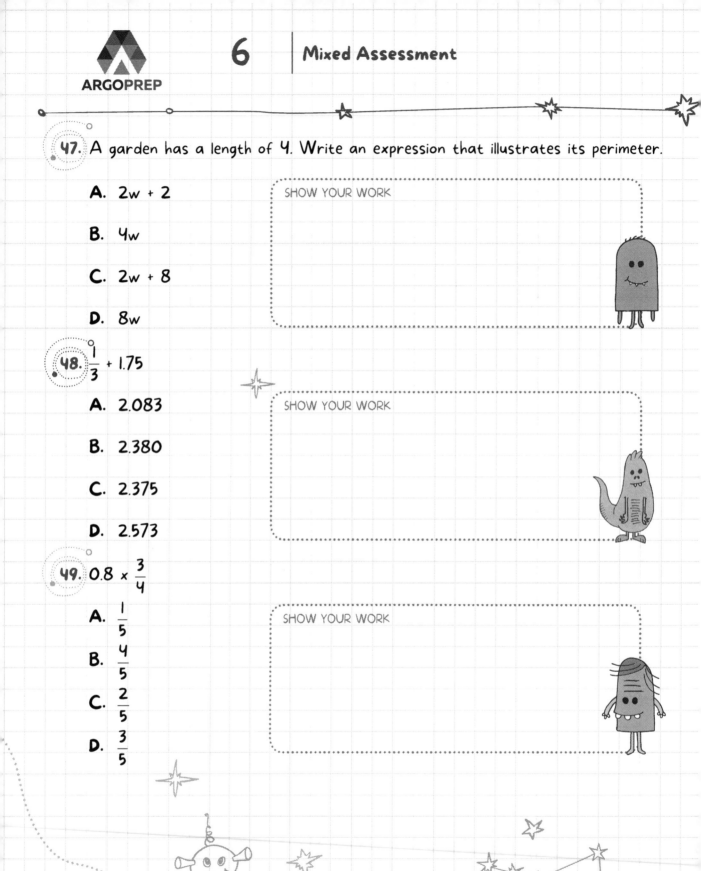

50. $2^3 + \dfrac{1}{2}(0.4 + 3.2)$

A. 4.2

B. 6.4

C. 7.8

D. 9.8

SHOW YOUR WORK

51. $15\left(4^2 \div 0.5 - 1\dfrac{1}{4}\right)$

A. $461\dfrac{1}{2}$

B. $461\dfrac{1}{4}$

C. $461\dfrac{3}{4}$

D. $461\dfrac{1}{5}$

SHOW YOUR WORK

52. $6x - 11 = 25$

A. $x = 6$

B. $x = 5$

C. $x = 4$

D. $x = 3$

SHOW YOUR WORK

ARGOPREP

53. $\dfrac{17-x}{3} = 5$

A. $x = 4$

B. $x = 3$

C. $x = 2$

D. $x = 1$

SHOW YOUR WORK

54. $3y + 4 = -5$

A. $y = 1$

B. $y = -1$

C. $y = 3$

D. $y = -3$

SHOW YOUR WORK

55. $\dfrac{x+9}{12} = 3$

A. $x = 11$

B. $x = 36$

C. $x = 16$

D. $x = 27$

SHOW YOUR WORK

56. $-3y + 11 > 14$

   A. $y > -1$

   B. $y > 1$

   C. $y < -1$

   D. $y < 1$

SHOW YOUR WORK

57. $6y - 12 < -6$

   A. $y < -1$

   B. $y < 1$

   C. $y > -1$

   D. $y > 1$

SHOW YOUR WORK

58. Jaden spends **\$120** buying clothes. He spent $\frac{1}{2}$ of his money on pants and the rest on shirts and a hat. If the hat was **\$11.50** and he bought 2 shirts, how much was each shirt?

   A. \$20.24

   B. \$23.25

   C. \$24.25

   D. \$25.24

SHOW YOUR WORK

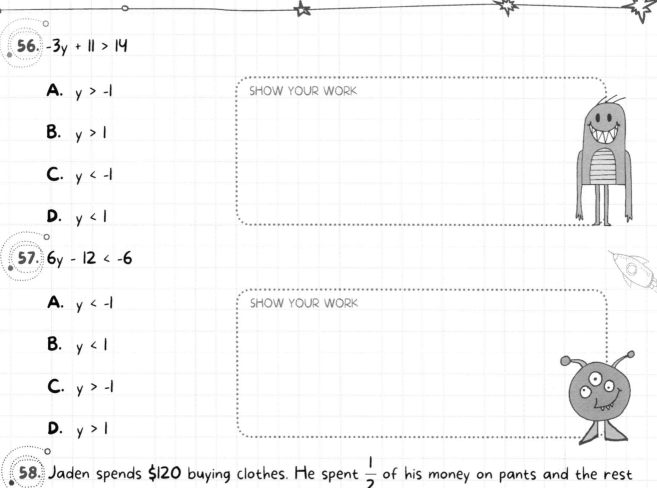

59. A garden has an area of 40. If it's length is 8, which equation represents its width?

A. 8w = 40

B. 5w = 40

C. 5 + w = 40

D. w - 8 = 40

SHOW YOUR WORK

60. Rianna is saving her allowance for a computer. She saves to raise $25 each month. Which inequality can be used to determine the number of months, m, Rianna must save to meet a goal of $800?

A. 25m > 800

B. 25m< 800

C. m+25 >800

D. 800m< 25

SHOW YOUR WORK

61. Tony draws a map of the Mississippi River. In the scale Tony uses on his map, **2** centimeters represents **50** miles. The actual length of the Rio Grande is around **2350** miles. The river Tony starts to draw on his map is **10** centimeters.

How many more centimeters should Tony add to the river on his map so it is an accurate model of the Mississippi?

A. 37

B. 3.5

C. 23.5

D. 84

SHOW YOUR WORK

62. Hexagon ABCDEF is a regular polygon with a perimeter of **19.2** inches.   Hexagon JKLMNO is **4** times larger and similar to Hexagon ABCDEF.

How long is each side of Hexagon JKLMNO?

A. 16.4

B. 4.2

C. 12.8

D. 8.9

SHOW YOUR WORK

63. If side MP measures 6.4 inches, what does side FJ measure?

F   G

4.4 in.

J   H

M   5.6 in.   N

3.2 in.

P   O

A. 8 in

B. 4 in

C. 6.4 in

D. 10 in

SHOW YOUR WORK

64. Which triangle has angle measures of **90°**, **30°**, and **60°**

A. Obtuse

B. Acute

C. Right

D. Isosceles

SHOW YOUR WORK

65. Which angle measures represents an isosceles obtuse triangle?

A. 53°, 44°, 83°

B. 110°, 40°, 40°

C. 99°, 37°, 44°

D. 88°, 46°, 46°

SHOW YOUR WORK

66. Which triangle has angle measures of **27°, 68°, 85°**?

A. Obtuse

B. Acute

C. Right

D. Isosceles

SHOW YOUR WORK

67. Draw a triangle. The length of one leg is **4** cm, and the length of another leg is **2.5** cm. Measure the third leg and describe the triangle.

SHOW YOUR WORK

68. If you slice a rectangular pyramid in half vertically, what shape do you get?

A. Oval

B. Circle

C. Triangle

D. Rectangle

SHOW YOUR WORK

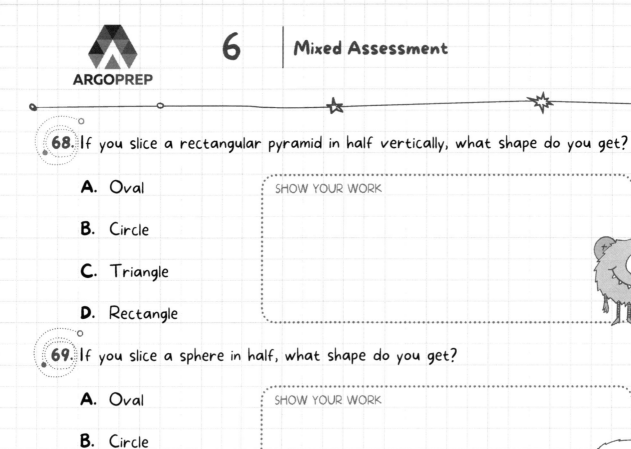

69. If you slice a sphere in half, what shape do you get?

A. Oval

B. Circle

C. Triangle

D. Rectangle

SHOW YOUR WORK

70. If you slice a rectangular prism in half horizontally, what shape do you get?

A. Oval

B. Circle

C. Triangle

D. Rectangle

SHOW YOUR WORK

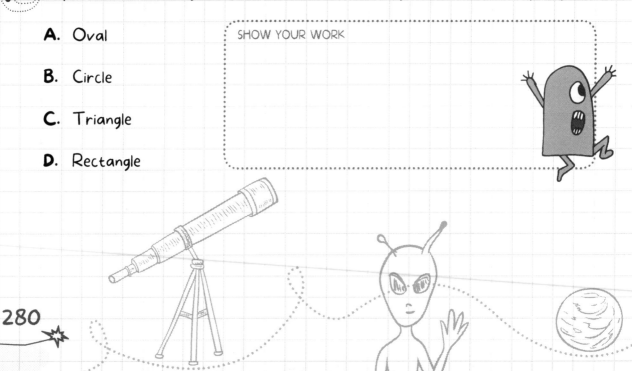

71. What is the circumference of a circle with radius of 7 in?

    A. 53.69 in

    B. 37. 96 in

    C. 43.96 in

    D. 21.98 in

SHOW YOUR WORK

72. What is the area of a circle with a diameter of 11 in?

    A. 25.14 in²

    B. 69.08 in²

    C. 94.99 in²

    D. 34.54 in²

SHOW YOUR WORK

73. What is the radius of a circle with a circumference of 107.76 cm?

    A. 17 cm

    B. 34 cm

    C. 7 cm

    D. 24 cm

SHOW YOUR WORK

74. What is the diameter of a circle with an area of 1519.76 m²?

A. 44 m

B. 22 m

C. 11 m

D. 14 m

SHOW YOUR WORK

75. What is the measurement of a complementary angle if it is paired with an angle that is 36°?

A. 144°

B. 54°

C. 84°

D. 64°

SHOW YOUR WORK

76. What is the measurement of a vertical angle if the other angle measures 39°?

A. 51°

B. 39°

C. 141°

D. 79°

SHOW YOUR WORK

ARGOPREP

77. What is the equation for an unknown angle if one angle in a pair of supplementary angles measures 114°?

A. a + 114 = 180

B. a - 114 = 180

C. 180 - a = a

D. 90 - a = 114

SHOW YOUR WORK

78. Maria wants to fill this box $\frac{1}{3}$ with sand and $\frac{2}{3}$ with water. How much space will the water occupy?

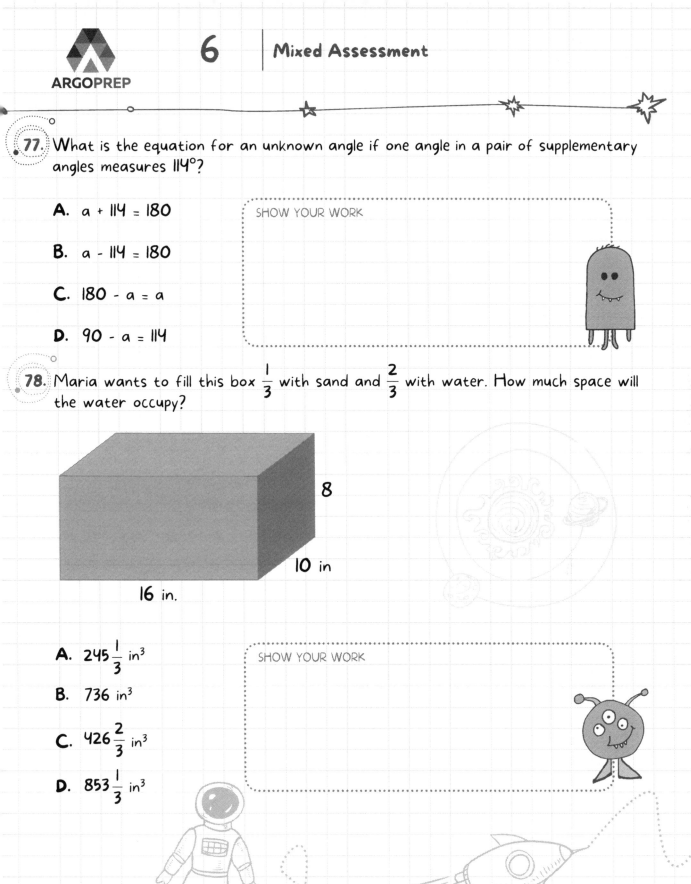

8

10 in

16 in.

A. $245\frac{1}{3}$ in³

B. 736 in³

C. $426\frac{2}{3}$ in³

D. $853\frac{1}{3}$ in³

SHOW YOUR WORK

79. Melissa wants to wrap this cylinder which has a height of 15 cm and a radius of 7 cm. How much wrapping paper does she need?

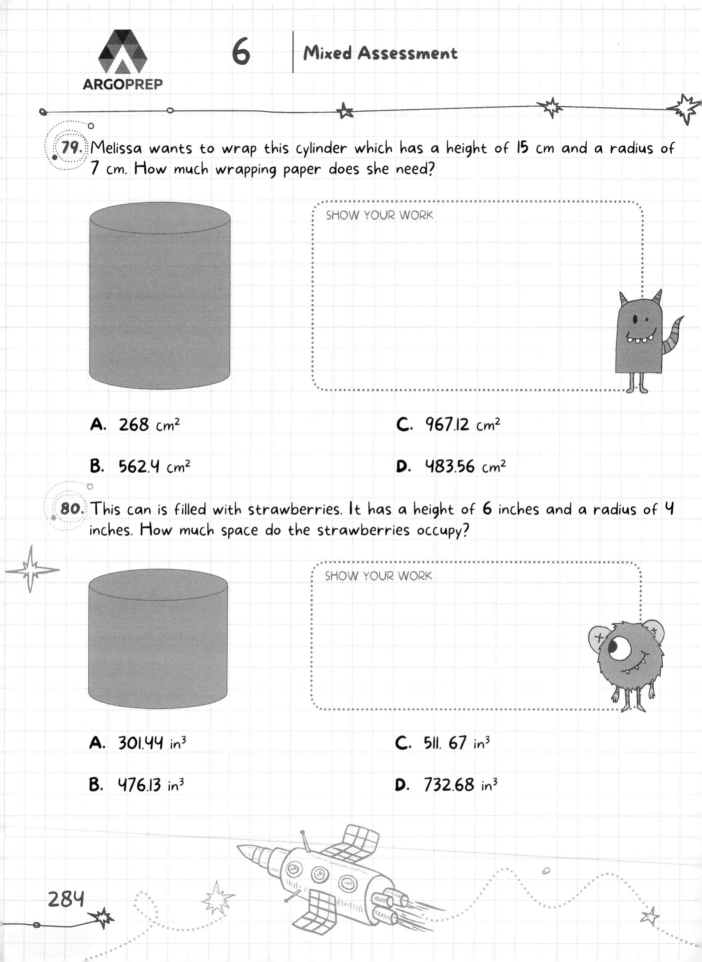

SHOW YOUR WORK

A. 268 cm²

C. 967.12 cm²

B. 562.4 cm²

D. 483.56 cm²

80. This can is filled with strawberries. It has a height of 6 inches and a radius of 4 inches. How much space do the strawberries occupy?

SHOW YOUR WORK

A. 301.44 in³

C. 511. 67 in³

B. 476.13 in³

D. 732.68 in³

81. Conner takes a train from New York City to Washington D.C. There are **85** passengers on the train. Conner determines **76%** of the passengers are men. Which response describes a random sample Conner could have used to make this prediction?

A. Conner counted the first eight people on the train.

B. Conner counted the person in the aisle seat of each aisle.

C. Conner asked the women how many men there are.

D. Conner counted all the men on the train.

SHOW YOUR WORK

82. Jose places **200** marbles inside a bag. The marbles are blue, black, green and red. After drawing a marble out of the bag **50** times, he takes out **7** black marbles, 1 blue marble, **35** red marbles, and **7** green marbles. Based on his sample, about how many marbles in the bag are blue?

A. 40

B. 2

C. 4

D. 6

SHOW YOUR WORK

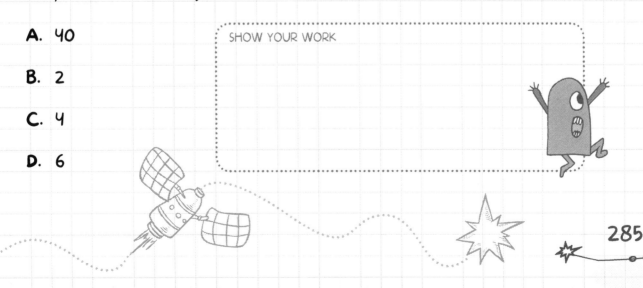

83. Jose places **200** marbles inside a bag. The marbles are blue, black, green and red. After drawing a marble out of the bag **50** times, he takes out **7** black marbles, **1** blue marble, **35** red marbles, and **7** green marbles. Based on his sample, about how many marbles in the bag are purple?

A. 10

B. 0

C. 100

D. 1

SHOW YOUR WORK

84. Beth collects data about a group of travelers' recent visit to Alaska. She records her data in this table.

Level of Satisfaction with Visit	Number of People
1 - Unsatisfied	15
2 - Somewhat satisfied	1
3 - Satisfied	2
4 - Very satisfied	7

SHOW YOUR WORK

What is a conclusion Beth can draw based on his data?

A. The majority of people were unsatisfied with their trip.

B. The majority of people were satisfied with their trip.

C. All people were unsatisfied about the trip.

D. The majority of people were undecided about their trip.

85. There are **600** students in Elijah's school. Using this data to make inferences about the entire school, how many students play soccer?

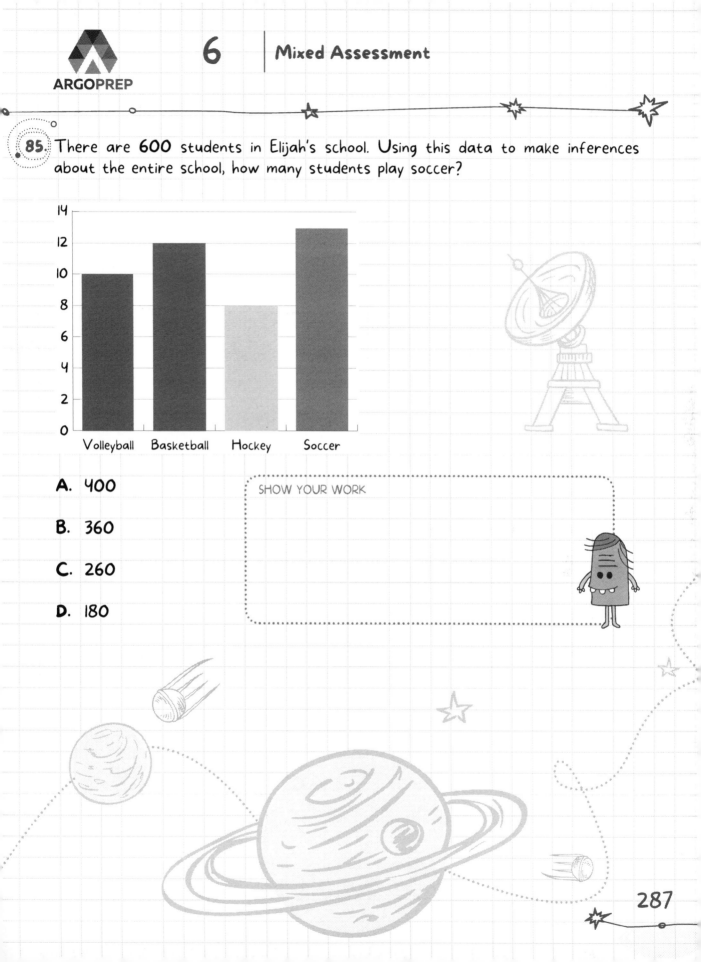

A. 400

B. 360

C. 260

D. 180

SHOW YOUR WORK

86. What is the statistical center of Ms Dhabis's class?

Ms. Smith's Class

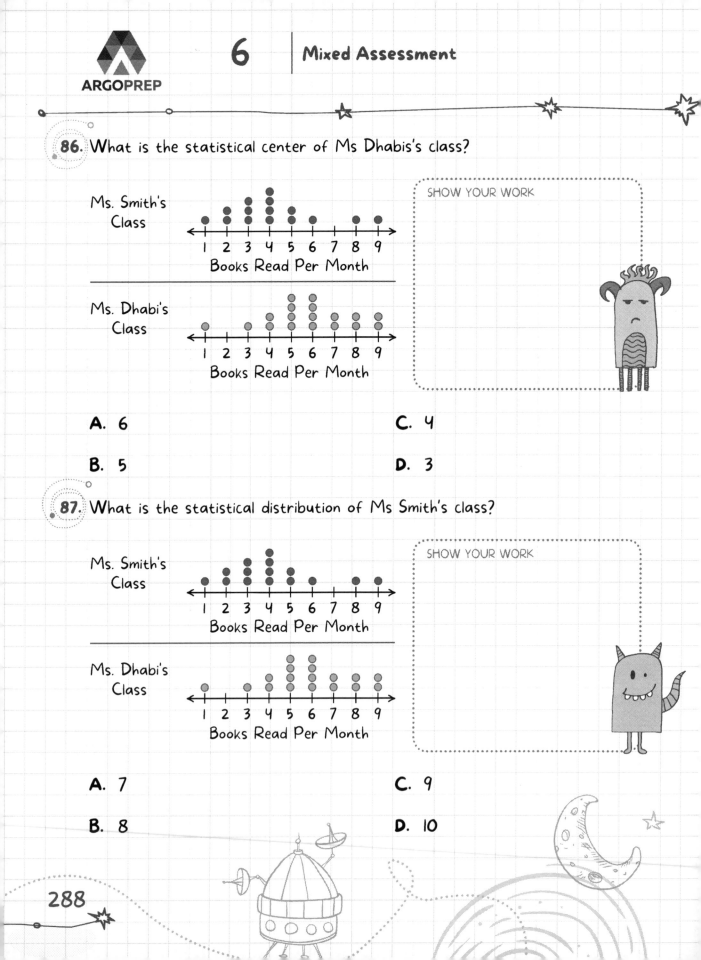

Books Read Per Month

SHOW YOUR WORK

Ms. Dhabi's Class

Books Read Per Month

A. 6   C. 4

B. 5   D. 3

87. What is the statistical distribution of Ms Smith's class?

Ms. Smith's Class

Books Read Per Month

SHOW YOUR WORK

Ms. Dhabi's Class

Books Read Per Month

A. 7   C. 9

B. 8   D. 10

88. Annalise is baking cookies. The values in this table list the amount of time it takes for each batch of cookies to bake. The batches take ?, 18, 19, 17 and 16 minutes. The mean for the batch is 17.4 minutes.

	Annalise's Cookies (minutes)
1st	?
2nd	18
3rd	19
4th	17
5th	16

SHOW YOUR WORK

How long did the first batch take?

A. 17 minutes

B. 16 minutes

C. 15 minutes

D. 215 minutes

89. Hannah surveys a random sample of 11 students at her school to find out how many students ride the bus. Seven students ride the bus. Which number is an appropriate prediction of the number of students in the school who ride the bus if there are 160 students at his school?

A. 59

B. 41

C. 102

D. 83

SHOW YOUR WORK

90. John has a bag with **25** marbles. There are **12** blue, **11** white, **1** black and **1** yellow marbles inside the bag. What is the probability of drawing a white marble from John's bag?

A. unlikely

B. impossible

SHOW YOUR WORK

C. neither unlikely or likely

D. certain

91. Edward flips a coin. The coin has heads on one side, and tails on the other. Edward flips the coin **50** times. Which value is an accurate prediction of the number of times Edward should expect to have the coin land on heads?

A. 25

B. 50

SHOW YOUR WORK

C. 75

D. 100

92. Martha is rolling a six-sided number cube **100** times. The numbers on the cube are the numbers 1-6. Which event is predicted to take place approximately **17** times?

A. Rolling 1-4

B. Rolling an even number

SHOW YOUR WORK

C. Rolling a 1

D. Rolling 2 or 3

93. Al flips a coin 10 times. He observes $\frac{6}{10}$ of his coin tosses result in a tails. Al combines his results with the other students in his class and discovers $\frac{6}{10}$ of the tosses for the entire class resulted in at least one tails.

How do the results of Al's class compare to the fraction of possible outcomes for rolling at least one five?

A. They are unrelated.

B. Equal to the possible outcomes

C. Higher than the possible outcomes

D. Lower than the possible outcomes

SHOW YOUR WORK

94. A number cube contains the numbers 1 through 6. Which probability model represents the chance of rolling a prime number on this number cube?

A. $\frac{5}{6}$

B. $\frac{2}{6}$

C. $\frac{1}{6}$

D. $\frac{1}{2}$

SHOW YOUR WORK

ARGOPREP

95. Roberta flips **2** coins. She records the possibilities of flipping each coin heads up, H, and tails up, T, in a list. Each coin flip is an independent event.
What is the probability of getting **2** heads?

A. $\frac{1}{4}$

B. $\frac{1}{8}$

C. $\frac{2}{4}$

D. $\frac{3}{6}$

SHOW YOUR WORK

96. Alex chooses a shirt, a pair of pants, and a pair of socks to wear to school each day. This table lists the color of each piece of clothing.

Shirt	Pants	Socks
White	Blue	White
Black	Khaki	Black
	Black	Tan

What is the probability that Alex will wear a white shirt?

A. $\frac{1}{2}$

B. $\frac{1}{8}$

C. $\frac{1}{3}$

D. $\frac{2}{5}$

SHOW YOUR WORK

97. Which data set has a mean of 7?

A. 4, 8, 7, 6

B. 3, 7, 7, 6

C. 3, 8, 11, 6

D. 7, 7, 8, 9, 13, 2

SHOW YOUR WORK

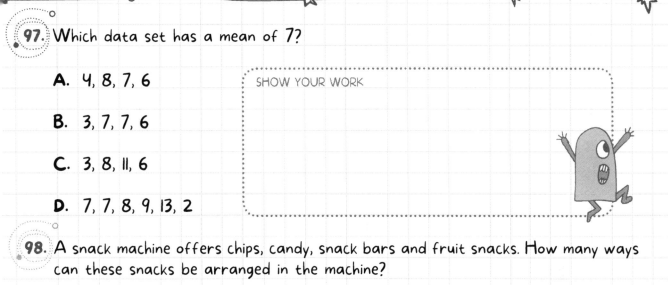

98. A snack machine offers chips, candy, snack bars and fruit snacks. How many ways can these snacks be arranged in the machine?

A. 28

B. 34

C. 32

D. 24

SHOW YOUR WORK

99. A jar contains 11 red beads, 6 green beads and 1 blue beads. What is the probability of selecting a red bead, replacing it, and then selecting a red bead?

A. 20%

B. 16%

C. 79%

D. 37%

SHOW YOUR WORK

100. A doctor is developing the patient schedule for next week. There are **3** new patients to be added to the schedule. In how many different orders could the patients be added to the schedule?

A. 5

B. 6

C. 7

D. 8

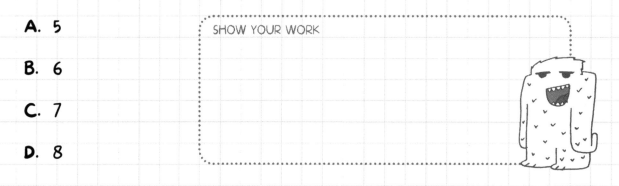

SHOW YOUR WORK

NOTES

ARGOPREP

NOTES

ANSWER SHEET

ANSWER SHEET

Chapter 1: Ratios & Proportional Relationships

1.1 Compute unit rates

1. The correct answer is D.
2. The correct answer is B.
3. The correct answer is C.
4. The correct answer is A.
5. The correct answer is B.
6. The correct answer is C.
7. The correct answer is D.
8. The correct answer is B.
9. The correct answer is A.
10. The correct answer is B.
11. The correct answer is C.
12. The correct answer is D.
13. The correct answer is A.
14. The correct answer is D.
15. The correct answer is C.
16. The correct answer is B.
17. The correct answer is B.
18. The correct answer is A.
19. The correct answer is D.
20. The correct answer is C.

1.2 Recognize and represent proportional relationships between quantities

1. The correct answer is A.
2. The correct answer is D.
3. The correct answer is B.
4. The correct answer is C.
5. The correct answer is A.
6. The correct answer is D.
7. The correct answer is B.
8. The correct answer is D.

ARGOPREP

9. The correct answer is C.
10. The correct answer is B.
11. The correct answer is D.
12. The correct answer is A.
13. The correct answer is A.
14. The correct answer is D.
15. The correct answer is C.
16. The correct answer is B.
17. The correct answer is A.
18. The correct answer is A.
19. The correct answer is C.
20. The correct answer is D.

1.3. Solving multi-step ratio and percent problems

1. The correct answer is B.
2. The correct answer is C.
3. The correct answer is D.
4. Correct response is No because he has to pay $13.20 in tax.
5. The correct answer is A.
6. The correct answer is B.
7. The correct answer is C.
8. The correct answer is C.
9. The correct answer is D.
10. The correct answer is B.
11. The correct answer is A.
12. The correct answer is D.
13. The correct answer is B.
14. The correct answer is C.
15. The correct answer is A.
16. The correct answer is B.
17. The correct answer is D.
18. The correct answer is C.
19. The correct answer is C.
20. The correct answer is A.

1.4. Chapter Test

1. The correct answer is D.
2. The correct answer is B.
3. The correct answer is A.
4. The correct answer is C.
5. The correct answer is B.
6. The correct answer is D.
7. The correct answer is C.
8. The correct answer is B.
9. The correct answer is C.
10. The correct answer is D.
11. The correct answer is B.
12. The correct answer is A.
13. The correct answer is D.
14. The correct answer is C.
15. The correct answer is D.
16. Correct answer is yes because his tax will only be $1.08.
17. The correct answer is B.
18. The correct answer is C.
19. The correct answer is A.
20. The correct answer is C.

Chapter 2: The Number System

2.1. Apply and extend previous understandings of operations with fractions

1. The correct answer is C.
2. The correct answer is B.
3. The correct answer is B.
4. The correct answer is D.
5. The correct answer is B.
6. The correct answer is D.

7. The correct answer is C.
8. The correct answer is A.
9. The correct answer is C.
10. The correct answer is B.
11. The correct answer is B.
12. The correct answer is D.
13. The correct answer is A.
14. The correct answer is C.
15. The correct answer is B.

2.2. Apply and extend previous understandings of multiplication and division

1. The correct answer is D.
2. The correct answer is A.
3. The correct answer is A.
4. The correct answer is C.
5. The correct answer is D.
6. The correct answer is A.
7. The correct answer is A.
8. The correct answer is B.
9. The correct answer is C.
10. The correct answer is C.
11. The correct answer is A.
12. The correct answer is B.
13. The correct answer is D.
14. The correct answer is C.
15. The correct answer is B.

2.3. Solve real-world problems involving the four operations

1. The correct answer is A.
2. The correct answer is D.
3. The correct answer is C.

4. The correct answer is B.
5. The correct answer is A.
6. The correct answer is D.
7. The correct answer is C.
8. The correct answer is A.
9. The correct answer is B.
10. The correct answer is D.
11. The correct answer is D.
12. The correct answer is A.
13. The correct answer is B.
14. The correct answer is C.
15. The correct answer is D.

2.4 Chapter Test

1. The correct answer is A.
2. The correct answer is C.
3. The correct answer is D.
4. The correct answer is B.
5. The correct answer is A.
6. The correct answer is C.
7. The correct answer is D.
8. The correct answer is B.
9. The correct answer is A.
10. The correct answer is D.
11. The correct answer is C.
12. The correct answer is B.
13. The correct answer is B.
14. The correct answer is A.
15. The correct answer is D.
16. The correct answer is C.
17. The correct answer is C.
18. The correct answer is A.
19. The correct answer is D.
20. The correct answer is C.

Chapter 3: Expressions and Equations

3.1.A Use properties of operations to generate equivalent expressions

1. The correct answer is D.
2. The correct answer is C.
3. The correct answer is B.
4. The correct answer is D.
5. The correct answer is A.
6. The correct answer is A.
7. The correct answer is B.
8. The correct answer is C.
9. The correct answer is A.
10. The correct answer is D.
11. The correct answer is C.
12. The correct answer is B.
13. The correct answer is A.
14. The correct answer is C.
15. The correct answer is B.
16. The correct answer is D.
17. The correct answer is C.
18. The correct answer is A.
19. The correct answer is B.
20. The correct answer is D.

3.1.B Use properties of operations to generate equivalent expressions

1. The correct answer is D.
2. The correct answer is B.
3. The correct answer is C.
4. The correct answer is A.
5. The correct answer is A.
6. The correct answer is B.
7. The correct answer is C.

8. The correct answer is D.
9. The correct answer is B.
10. The correct answer is C.
11. The correct answer is D.
12. The correct answer is A.
13. The correct answer is B.
14. The correct answer is C.
15. The correct answer is D.
16. The correct answer is A.
17. The correct answer is C.
18. The correct answer is B.
19. The correct answer is D.
20. The correct answer is C.

3.2.A Solve real-life and mathematical problems using numerical and algebraic expressions and equations

1. The correct answer is D.
2. The correct answer is D.
3. The correct answer is B.
4. The correct answer is A.
5. The correct answer is D.
6. The correct answer is D.
7. The correct answer is C.
8. The correct answer is B.
9. The correct answer is A.
10. The correct answer is C.
11. The correct answer is C.
12. The correct answer is A.
13. The correct answer is D.
14. The correct answer is B.
15. The correct answer is C.
16. Correct answer is yes. Students should show work that shows that John needs at least 21 people to attend and he will have at least 27 people attend.
17. The correct answer is A.

18. The correct answer is A.
19. The correct answer is B.
20. The correct answer is D.

3.2.B Solve real-life and mathematical problems using numerical and algebraic expressions and equations

1. The correct answer is A.
2. The correct answer is D.
3. The correct answer is C.
4. The correct answer is B.
5. The correct answer is B.
6. The correct answer is A.
7. The correct answer is C.
8. The correct answer is D.
9. The correct answer is A.
10. The correct answer is C.
11. The correct answer is D.
12. The correct answer is B.
13. The correct answer is A.
14. The correct answer is A.
15. Students should write the equation: $16x + 85 = 350$
16. The correct answer is B.
17. The correct answer is D.
18. The correct answer is $3.4 + x > 25$.
19. The correct answer is C.
20. The correct answer is B.

3.3 Chapter Test

1. The correct answer is A.
2. The correct answer is D.
3. The correct answer is C.
4. The correct answer is B.

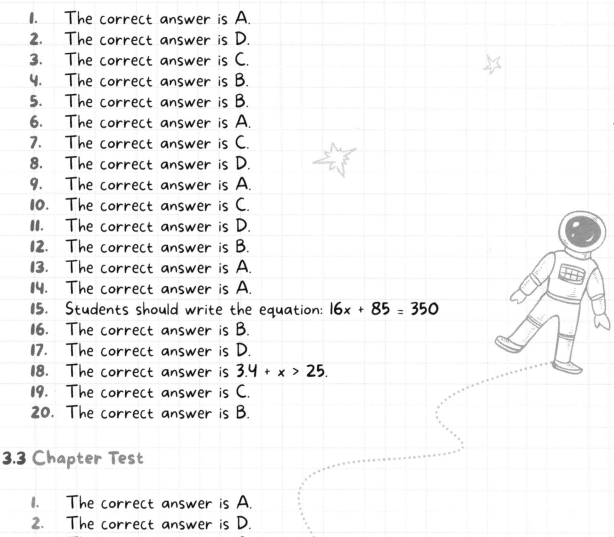

5. The correct answer is A.
6. The correct answer is D.
7. The correct answer is C.
8. The correct answer is B.
9. The correct answer is A.
10. The correct answer is C.
11. The correct answer is D.
12. The correct answer is B.
13. The correct answer is C.
14. The correct answer is A.
15. The correct answer is A.
16. Students should say the temperature should be less than 0°F because it rose 16° and was still below 0.
17. The correct answer is C.
18. The correct answer is B.
19. The correct answer is A.
20. The correct answer is B.

Chapter 4: Geometry

4.1.A Draw construct, and describe geometrical figures and describe the relationships between them

1. The correct answer is B.
2. The correct answer is C.
3. The correct answer is D.
4. The correct answer is A.
5. The correct answer is A.
6. The correct answer is B.
7. The correct answer is D.
8. The correct answer is no because there is only 11.875 feet between the dresser and bed.
9. The correct answer is A.
10. The correct answer is D.

11. The correct answer is A.
12. The correct answer is D.
13. The correct answer is C.
14. The correct answer is B.
15. The correct answer is A.

4.1.B Draw construct, and describe geometrical figures and describe the relationships between them

1. The correct answer is D.
2. The correct answer is C.
3. The correct answer is B.
4. The correct answer is A.
5. The correct answer is C.
6. The correct answer is A.
7. The correct answer is C.
8. The correct answer is B.
9. The correct answer is D.
10. Students should draw a triangle with sides of the appropriate length. Students should use measurements of sides and angles to justify their classification.
11. Students should construct a shape that is circular but has similar appearance to an egg. Student explanations should mention that it is a round figure but the line is not equidistant at all points of the shape.
12. Students should draw a shape that has 2 sets of parallel sides but not four equal sides. Their explanation should mention that their shape does not have four equal sides.
13. Students should draw a shape with four equal sides and explain it is a parallelogram because it has 2 sets of parallel sides.
14. Students should draw a shape with three unequal sides and one angle larger than 90°.
15. Students should draw a shape with eight sides.

4.1.C Draw construct, and describe geometrical figures and describe the relationships between them

1. The correct answer is D.
2. The correct answer is C.
3. The correct answer is C.
4. The correct answer is B.
5. The correct answer is D.
6. The correct answer is D.
7. The correct answer is A.
8. The correct answer is B.
9. The correct answer is C.
10. The correct answer is B.
11. The correct answer is A.
12. The correct answer is D.
13. Students should draw a three dimensional shape, resembling this

14. Students should draw a three dimensional shape, resembling this

15. Students should draw a three dimensional shape, resembling this

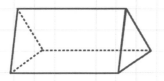

ANSWER SHEET

ARGOPREP

4.2.A Solve real-life and mathematical problems involving angle measure, area, surface area, and volume

1. The correct answer is A.
2. The correct answer is A.
3. The correct answer is C.
4. The correct answer is B.
5. The correct answer is D.
6. The correct answer is C.
7. The correct answer is C.
8. The correct answer is B.
9. The correct answer is D.
10. The correct answer is D.
11. The correct answer is D.
12. The correct answer is C.
13. The correct answer is A.
14. The correct answer is B.
15. The correct answer is D.

4.2.B Solve real-life and mathematical problems involving angle measure, area, surface area, and volume

1. The correct answer is A.
2. The correct answer is D.
3. The correct answer is D.
4. The correct answer is C.
5. The correct answer is B.
6. The correct answer is A.
7. The correct answer is A.
8. The correct answer is B.
9. The correct answer is C.
10. The correct answer is D.
11. The correct answer is C.

ANSWER SHEET

12. The correct answer is B.
13. The correct answer is A.
14. The correct answer is C.
15. The correct answer is D.

4.2.C Solve real-life and mathematical problems involving angle measure, area, surface area, and volume

1. The correct answer is B.
2. The correct answer is B.
3. The correct answer is D.
4. The correct answer is C.
5. The correct answer is A.
6. The correct answer is A.
7. The correct answer is D.
8. The correct answer is C.
9. The correct answer is B.
10. The correct answer is D.
11. The correct answer is D.
12. The correct answer is A.
13. The correct answer is A.
14. The correct answer is D.
15. The correct answer is **216** cm³. One possible way to find the total volume is to break the figure into **3** shapes, two triangular prisms and one rectangular prism.

4.3. Chapter Test

1. The correct answer is C.
2. The correct answer is C.
3. The correct answer is B.
4. The correct answer is A.
5. The correct answer is A.
6. Students should draw a triangle with three sides and label it with the appropriate name based on the measurements of the three sides.
7. The correct answer is D.

8. The correct answer is B.
9. The correct answer is C.
10. The correct answer is C.
11. The correct answer is B.
12. The correct answer is D.
13. The correct answer is D.
14. The correct answer is C.
15. The correct answer is B.
16. The correct answer is A.
17. The correct answer is D.
18. The correct answer is B.
19. The correct answer is A.
20. The correct answer is C.

Chapter 5: Statistics & Probability

5.1.A Use random sampling to draw inferences about a population

1. The correct answer is D.
2. The correct answer is C.
3. The correct answer is B.
4. The correct answer is A.
5. The correct answer is B.
6. The correct answer is C.
7. The correct answer is B.
8. The correct answer is C.
9. The correct answer is B.
10. The correct answer is B.
11. The correct answer is C.
12. The correct answer is A.
13. The correct answer is D.
14. This is a sample statistic because the results are based on the amount of teenagers surveyed not the amount of teenagers in the general population.
15. No, because he did **2** marbles are not representative of **30** marbles.

ANSWER SHEET

5.1.B Use random sampling to draw inferences about a population

1. The correct answer was A.
2. The correct answer was B.
3. The correct answer was D.
4. The correct answer was C.
5. The correct answer was C.
6. The correct answer was A.
7. The correct answer was B.
8. The correct answer was D.
9. The correct answer was C.
10. The correct answer was C.
11. The correct answer was D.
12. The correct answer was B.
13. The correct answer was A.
14. The correct answer was D.
15. One possible answer is yes because 4 x 10 is 40.

5.2.A Draw informal comparative inferences about two populations

1. The correct answer is D.
2. The correct answer is C.
3. The correct answer is A.
4. The correct answer is B.
5. The correct answer is A.
6. The correct answer is D.
7. The correct answer is A.
8. The correct answer is C.
9. The correct answer is A.
10. The correct answer is C.
11. The correct answer is D.
12. The correct answer is A.
13. The correct answer is B.
14. The correct answer is D.
15. The correct answer is C.

5.2.B Draw informal comparative inferences about two populations

1. The correct answer is D.
2. The correct answer is C.
3. The correct answer is A.
4. The correct answer is B.
5. The correct answer is B.
6. The correct answer is A.
7. The correct answer is D.
8. The correct answer is D.
9. The correct answer is A.
10. The correct answer is C.
11. The correct answer is B.
12. The correct answer is A.
13. The correct answer is D.
14. The correct answer is C.
15. The correct answer is A.

5.3.A Investigate chance processes and develop, use, and evaluate probability models

1. The correct answer is A.
2. The correct answer is B.
3. The correct answer is C.
4. The correct answer is D.
5. The correct answer is C.
6. The correct answer is A.
7. The correct answer is B.
8. The correct answer is D.
9. The correct answer is D.
10. The correct answer is C.
11. The correct answer is B.
12. The correct answer is B.
13. The correct answer is C.
14. The correct answer is A.
15. The correct answer is A.

5.3.B Investigate chance processes and develop, use, and evaluate probability models

1. The correct answer is A.
2. The correct answer is C.
3. The correct answer is D.
4. The correct answer is B.
5. The correct answer is B.
6. The correct answer is A.
7. The correct answer is C.
8. The correct answer is B.
9. The correct answer is B.
10. The correct answer is D.
11. The correct answer is C.
12. The correct answer is A.
13. The correct answer is B.
14. The correct answer is D.
15. The correct answer is A.

5.3.C Investigate chance processes and develop, use, and evaluate probability models

1. The correct answer is C.
2. The correct answer is C.
3. The correct answer is D.
4. The correct answer is B.
5. The correct answer is B.
6. The correct answer is C.
7. The correct answer is A.
8. The correct answer is B.
9. The correct answer is C.
10. The correct answer is C.

11. The correct answer is B.
12. The correct answer is D.
13. The correct answer is A.
14. Student lists should all possible combinations of each shirt, pants and socks.
15. Students should explain they calculate the probability or drawing a consonant and then multiply it by the probability of drawing an S.

5.4 Chapter Test

1. The correct answer is A.
2. The correct answer is D.
3. The correct answer is B.
4. The correct answer is C.
5. The correct answer is D.
6. The correct answer is B.
7. The correct answer is A.
8. The correct answer is C.
9. The correct answer is A.
10. The correct answer is D.
11. The correct answer is C.
12. The correct answer is A.
13. The correct answer is C.
14. The correct answer is D.
15. The correct answer is B.
16. The correct answer is C.
17. The correct answer is A.
18. The correct answer is D.
19. The correct answer is C.
20. The correct answer is B.

Chapter 6: Final Assessment

1. The correct answer is D.
2. The correct answer is B.

ANSWER SHEET

3. The correct answer is A.
4. The correct answer is A.
5. The correct answer is C.
6. The correct answer is B.
7. The correct answer is D.
8. The correct answer is A.
9. The correct answer is B.
10. The correct answer is A.
11. The correct answer is C.
12. The correct answer is D.
13. The correct answer is C.
14. The correct answer is C.
15. The correct answer is A.
16. Correct answer: Yes, because with tax, the groceries will cost $81.90.
17. The correct answer is B.
18. The correct answer is C.
19. The correct answer is A.
20. The correct answer is A.
21. The correct answer is D.
22. The correct answer is C.
23. The correct answer is C.
24. The correct answer is B.
25. The correct answer is B.
26. The correct answer is A.
27. The correct answer is C.
28. The correct answer is A.
29. The correct answer is D.
30. The correct answer is C.
31. The correct answer is A.
32. The correct answer is B.
33. The correct answer is A.
34. Students should create a number line and place a marker on -6. Then, they should draw 4 arrows to the left and end on -10.
35. Students should create a number line and place a marker on -4. Then, they should draw 5 arrows to the right and end on 1.

ANSWER SHEET

36. The correct answer is C.
37. The correct answer is B.
38. The correct answer is D.
39. The correct answer is A.
40. The correct answer is A.
41. The correct answer is A.
42. The correct answer is C.
43. The correct answer is D.
44. The correct answer is B.
45. The correct answer is A.
46. The correct answer is C.
47. The correct answer is C.
48. The correct answer is A.
49. The correct answer is D.
50. The correct answer is D.
51. The correct answer is B.
52. The correct answer is A.
53. The correct answer is C.
54. The correct answer is D.
55. The correct answer is D.
56. The correct answer is C.
57. The correct answer is B.
58. The correct answer is C.
59. The correct answer is A.
60. The correct answer is A.
61. The correct answer is D.
62. The correct answer is C.
63. The correct answer is A.
64. The correct answer is C.
65. The correct answer is B.
66. The correct answer is B.
67. Students should draw a shape with three sides and show each sides measurement. Students should also describe their triangle using the proper term based on its sides.

ARGOPREP

68. The correct answer is C.
69. The correct answer is B.
70. The correct answer is D.
71. The correct answer is C.
72. The correct answer is C.
73. The correct answer is A.
74. The correct answer is A.
75. The correct answer is B.
76. The correct answer is B.
77. The correct answer is A.
78. The correct answer is D.
79. The correct answer is C.
80. The correct answer is A.
81. The correct answer is B.
82. The correct answer is C.
83. The correct answer is B.
84. The correct answer is A.
85. The correct answer is D.
86. The correct answer is A.
87. The correct answer is B.
88. The correct answer is A.
89. The correct answer is C.
90. The correct answer is C.
91. The correct answer is A.
92. The correct answer is C.
93. The correct answer is A.
94. The correct answer is D.
95. The correct answer is A.
96. The correct answer is A.
97. The correct answer is C.
98. The correct answer is D.
99. The correct answer is D.
100. The correct answer is B.

Made in the USA
Lexington, KY
28 July 2019